Doing December Dif

An alternative Christmas handbook

Doing December Differently

An alternative Christmas handbook

Nicola Slee & Rosie Miles

WILD GOOSE PUBLICATIONS

www.ionabooks.com

First published 2006, reprinted 2008, 2011

Wild Goose Publications, 4th Floor, Savoy House, 140 Sauchiehall St, Glasgow G2 3DH, UK.
Wild Goose Publications is the publishing division of the Iona Community.
Scottish Charity No. SC003794. Limited Company Reg. No. SC096243.
www.ionabooks.com

ISBN 978-1-905010-23-3

Cover photograph © Armands Erglis

The publishers gratefully acknowledge the support of the Drummond Trust,
3 Pitt Terrace, Stirling FK8 2EY in producing this book.

A catalogue record for this book is available from the British Library.

Overseas distribution:
Australia: Willow Connection Pty Ltd, Unit 4A, 3-9 Kenneth Road, Manly Vale, NSW 2093
New Zealand: Pleroma, Higginson Street, Otane 4170, Central Hawkes Bay
Canada: Novalis/Bayard Publishing & Distribution, 10 Lower Spadina Avenue, Suite 400, Toronto, Ontario M5V 2Z3

Printed by Bell & Bain, Thornliebank, Glasgow

To the Cropthorne six:

*Kate Fyfe, Peter Kettle, Kate Lees,
Ailsa McLaren, Anne Pounds and Sue Tompkins,
with love and thanks,*

*and with thanks to Holland House, Cropthorne,
for enabling it to happen*

Contents

Introduction

Spirit of Christmas
pity our wandering
bring us back home

Pat Pinsent

For many people, the Christmas 'season' (which starts around September) is a highly ambivalent time. In the West it has become a mega fest of conspicuous consumption an excessive, prolonged and often frenetic period of spending, feasting, jollifications and exchanging of gifts and greetings, which leaves us at best stressed, and at worst under intolerable strain. Perhaps this has some deep roots, in the Northern hemisphere, in the need for a festival of light and warmth at the time of winter solstice: as nature asserts her powers of darkness and cold, humans assert their will to life by gathering around fires, lighting candles and filling their bellies against the bitter season. Although still maintaining some ancient religious roots, as a secular festival Christmas has largely been shorn from its biblical and liturgical context and has lost the rich and subversive range of meanings it holds within the Christian narrative. Only a few liturgically minded purists maintain any sense of the larger rhythm of the Christmas season – the 40-day period starting with Advent and moving through Christmas to Epiphany and climaxing in Candlemas, a season marking and exploring in profound depths the mystery of God's incarnation in the birth and life of Jesus Christ.

As part of the preparation for this book, a survey of three church congregations was undertaken to explore attitudes towards and feelings about Christmas. As might be expected, a variety of perspectives and views was expressed, from those who associate the season with exhaustion and a gritted determination to 'get through', on the one hand, to those who regard it as a time of heightened spiritual significance and celebration of the love of family and friends, on the other. Here are some comments that people made:

> 'At best this is a time to stop, take stock, remember friends near and far, as well as a time to indulge in a certain form of hibernation (eating and enjoying fine food, then not going out much or doing much for several days). Somehow that does feel befitting of the time of year.'

> 'Christmas at the moment equals exhaustion.'

> 'The celebration of the winter solstice predates Christianity by many centuries, and no amount of do-gooding will alter the inbred need to whoop it up in the depths of winter.'

> 'Our family is not Christian or churchgoing and to make Christmas a spiritual event would exclude family, so I tend to see it as a family opportunity and go with the flow.'

'I struggle to keep the birth of the human face of God at the heart of things. Everything else is a by-product, some of it very good, other bits increasingly repellent.'

'If Christmas was taken away, how dull it would be. It is the climax of the year, and well worth preserving as it is very meaningful and necessary both spiritually and physically.'

'Christmas should be brief and beautiful – all the rest is vanity.'

'Christmas is a difficult Christian festival because it has always been a blend of pre-Christian celebration with a Christian overlay. It is easy to feel that the pre-Christian is swamping the Christian, especially in our secular society – but a bit difficult to complain about this when we infiltrated the existing celebrations (Saturnalia, Yule, etc …)!'

'If the incarnate God means anything, it means – among many other things – celebrating physical elements (food, decorations, etc) as a manifestation of the spiritual. So we should not feel uncomfortable about the physical and material aspects of Christmas but use them to express and share joy.'

'People love it. I'm sure God appreciates the attention as well!'

These very mixed views reflect something of the tensions that most people we have spoken to experience in relation to the phenomenon of Christmas.

The media and advertising sell the season as a paean to an idealised notion of the nuclear family, in which children are made central and yet, paradoxically, their deepest needs are all too easily overlooked. The pressure on parents to buy the latest toys, gadgets and fads is immense. Those with little spare cash can find themselves in debt if they spend, and feeling inadequate if they don't. Christmas puts an intolerable strain on millions of families, a fair number of whom no longer conform to the traditional pattern of two partners (of different genders) married to each other and living under the one roof, with shared offspring. In Britain, much more than in other European countries, public life seems to close down for an extended period at Christmas, with businesses, shops, museums and galleries shutting their doors, and only limited public services carrying on as usual. Families are left to fend for themselves and to feed on each other's company, without escape or support from outside the home. Many cannot sustain this pressure, and it is a well-known fact that there are more instances of domestic violence, family breakdown and murder at Christmas than at any other time of year.

With its compulsive idolatry of money and consumption, and its idealisation of family life, the way our culture celebrates Christmas marginalises and excludes great numbers of people. These include anyone from any kind of broken or dysfunctional family (and that includes most of us); single people, whether by choice or circumstance; those who are divorced or separated; childless couples who long for children; bereaved parents or parents of profoundly sick children; children who, for whatever reasons, do not fit the mould of active, acquisitive consumers; gay, lesbian, bisexual and transgendered folk. All are ostracised from the mythical idyll of Christmas, unable to play happy families.

Christmas is also deeply problematic for all of us who cannot or do not wish to comply with the pressures of materialism that the secular season exerts. Poorer people cannot play this game; and many others of us don't want to. Christians often find themselves caught in the dilemma of wanting to mark the feast in some meaningful way consonant with the spirit of the festival, but abhorring the greed, consumerism and meaningless conviviality which the culture seems to impose. But it is not only Christians who want to live by other values and maintain a lifestyle of simplicity, generosity and care for the outsider. People of all faiths and none struggle with the conundrum of resisting the massive market pressures to spend, buy and consume at Christmas. How too does one respond to Christmas as a believing Jew or Muslim in contemporary Britain – or as a convinced humanist or atheist?

Doing December Differently seeks to address these and other such issues and questions. How might we resist and protest against the wasteful excesses of the Christmas season without being puritanical killjoys? How might we protest against the myopia of cultural consumerism that blinds us to the larger demands of global poverty and injustice, and find ways of celebrating Christmas that are truly good news for the poor and disadvantaged? How might we acknowledge our connections with family members, friends and others who have been and are significant to us, in ways that are life-giving and joyful, rather than compulsive and draining? What rites, rituals and ceremonies might we use to help us mark out the days and nights of this midwinter season that are meaningful to us today, drawing on ancient roots but also minting fresh language, fresh gestures, fresh meanings? How might we do December (and the months leading up to and away from it) differently?

Through the stories and reflections of more than eighty contributors from within and beyond Christian tradition, this book explores how people of faith and goodwill might mark the midwinter season and the Christmas festival (not, of course, the same thing) with integrity and simplicity, in ways that include others and celebrate difference, that do not put us all under intolerable strain, or perpetuate false and oppressive myths of the ideal family life. We seek to offer resources that demonstrate how Christmas might be marked in more moderate, yet genuinely celebratory ways that respect and enact core spiritual values. Although the majority of pieces have been written from a Christian perspective, we have deliberately sought to include other voices. We hope that those of other faiths and none may find clues here towards how to participate in British society at this point of the year without feeling obliterated or coerced into patterns of behaviour that tell lies about who and what they are. Rabbi Michael Lerner, of the Network of Spiritual Progressives, writes powerfully of the potential universal appeal of the Christmas season in the following terms:

> There is a beautiful spiritual message underlying Christmas that has universal appeal: the hope that gets reborn in moments of despair, the light that gets re-lit in the darkest moments of the year, is beautifully symbolised by the story of a child born of a teenage homeless mother who had to give birth in a manger because no one would give her shelter, and escaping the cruelty of Roman imperial rule and its local surrogate, Herod, who already knew that such a child would grow up to challenge the entire imperialist system. To celebrate that vulnerable child as a symbol of hope that eventually the weak would triumph over the rule of the arrogant and powerful is a spiritual celebration with strong analogies to our Jewish Chanukah celebration, which also cele-brates the victory of the weak over the powerful. And many other spiritual traditions around the world have similar celebrations at this time of year.

The genesis of the book

The idea for this book had its genesis in a particular Christmas gathering a few years ago. Nicola and her good friend Peter Kettle had, over the years, often reflected on the dilemma of how to mark and celebrate Christmas as (then) single people who, for various reasons, did not want to return to their parental homes every year. They had shared one memorable Christmas in Bruges, and perhaps it was then they hatched the idea of 'doing an alternative Christmas': self-consciously and intention-ally seeking to create, with others, a way of marking the Christmas season that went against the grain of mainstream social custom. So, in 2000, they invited a group of friends to make Christmas with them at Holland House, a lovely timbered retreat house in the village of Cropthorne, near Pershore, Worcestershire. We were a group of eight, all female (apart from Peter), all childless, all either single and/or lesbian/gay – all of us people who had struggled to know what to do and where to go at Christmas.

We came together at the beginning of Christmas week. First of all we spent time sharing our own mixed memories of, and thoughts and feelings about, Christmas. We brainstormed what we liked about Christmas and what we hated about Christ-mas. We spoke about what we wanted from this special time together, seeking to hold together different needs and hopes. We became aware, as the week progressed, of the intense feelings around for each of us at this time of the year which, for most people, is imbued with deep childhood memories and powerful associations. At various times in the week, quite a few of us shed tears, felt lost – unsure of ourselves or of why we had come – and wondered if it wouldn't have been less painful to have forgotten the whole enterprise. At the same time, there was an immense creative buzz about being together and trying something different, an explosion of positive

Christmas loves and hates

A brainstorm from the Cropthorne Christmas

HATES	LOVES
Waste	Food
Politeness	Christmas lights
Expectations of false jollity	Tinsel and glitter
Long letters about children's exploits	Candles and bells
Family pressures	The growing darkness
Lost families	The power of the dark
People's pity/sympathy	Being alone
'Christmas is for children'	Being with others
It starts in September	The joy and delight of children
Loss of rhythm, sense of seasons	Supported solitude
Excessive spending, eating, drinking –	Treats – mince pies, stuffed dates
and public display of same	Aspects of the biblical stories –
Christmas in the workplace	e.g. the vulnerable child
Trapped into complying	Care of the outsider, stranger, and poor
Not able to think of alternatives	Special presents from people who care
Plastic rubbish	People being in touch; connections
Disney culture	Re-establishing connections
Exploitation	Eliminating tit for tat cards
Hackneyed food	Watching TV by the fire
Difficulty in finding any religious meaning	Going abroad
Having one's own reality denied	Being with conducive people
Doctrinal orthodox rubbish	Silence and contemplation
Fantasy	Midnight mass
Sentimentality	Rediscovering things from childhood
Being manipulated	Christmas trees
Torn between competing family claims	Smells, e.g. wood burning, spices
A lonely time	Mulled wine
Rootlessness	Advent music
Travel: nightmares on motorway and trains	Christmas carols – at the right time
Price hiking	Handmade gifts
Tit for tat Christmas cards and presents	People's generosity
Rubbish on TV	Playing games
Being a vicar at Christmas	Going for walks
Drunkenness	Staying at home
Falseness and hypocrisy	The best part is after all the hype is over

energy, much laughing and genuine comedy amidst the tears. We made a pattern of our days in which we had plenty of free time to be alone or to team up in twos or threes to walk, talk, play games, watch TV. We planned a week's menu of simple winter fare, with special meals on Christmas Eve and Christmas Day, and took it in turns to prepare food in pairs. We sang carols around the piano in the chapel, read each other poems, circle danced, joked and gave each other massage. We gathered together briefly at the end of each day to share any thoughts, feelings or concerns about how we were experiencing the time together.

At the heart of the week was our own liturgy, which we created in pairings or threesomes: simple, 'homemade' rituals that, in different ways, named our experiences of ambivalent belonging on the edges of Christian tradition and traditional family life; our longings for home and acceptance; our desire for God or the holy, however we chose to name this mystery; our sense of duty to care for the stranger; our celebration of networks of friendships that sustained our lives. These and other themes, arising out of reflection on our own experiences of Christmases past, were forged into prayerful words, gestures and symbolic acts. The moods held together by these liturgies encompassed anger and mourning, longing and desire, joy and thanksgiving. (Some of these liturgies, as well as personal stories from the week, appear at various points in this book.)

It was an enormously powerful and significant time for each of us. There was something healing and cathartic about being able to name and explore, in a company of trusted companions, our sense of ambivalence about and exclusion from the central social and religious rites of Christmas with which we had grown up. There was great release and creativity in making our own liturgy, shaping our days and nights and patterning our time together in ways that made sense of who and what we were, in ways that recognised our hurts and wounds as well as our gifts and the blessings we brought one another. We did something creative together with a time and a social rite that had, in the past, often been problematic for us, and, in doing so, helped to wrest the oppressive power of Christmas from its place in our psyches, and created something life-giving and good. Although the week itself was its own thing and, we felt, not to be repeated, nevertheless it seemed to hold a significance beyond the gathering of this particular group of eight. The energy and ideas it generated around 'doing Christmas differently' have outlived the particular occasion and given birth to this book.

Shape and format

The book is divided into three main sections. Part one consists of personal stories, poems and reflections from individuals telling their experiences of Christmas, naming what can be difficult and problematic as well as celebrating the gifts and graces of the season. Whilst by no means containing all the kinds of stories that could be told about Christmas, these chapters do offer a wide range of voices that can challenge us all to think about the season in different ways.

Part two moves on to a consideration of how to 'do December differently'. Before turning to concrete suggestions, we offer a series of historical, liturgical, theological and sociological reflections about the origins, diverse meanings and customs associated with Christmas, which are intended to provide a context in which to think about the pragmatics of how to 'do' the season differently.

Part three consists of liturgical and ritual resources: prayers, poems and liturgies organised around various themes. These chapters contain a wide variety of creative materials that can be adapted and used in the home, in group gatherings, in church settings and in other contexts.

Thanks and acknowledgements

Very many people have contributed to this book. We owe an obvious debt to all the people who contributed pieces, not all of which have made it into print. Many others talked to us about Christmas and their loves and hates associated with the season. Some recommended books to read, websites to search and ideas to explore. Members of three church congregations took part in a survey of attitudes towards Christmas which we have drawn on in planning this book, and we thank the clergy and laity of the three parishes concerned (one in Birmingham and two in London). We are grateful to our editors at Wild Goose Publications who have been helpful and encouraging at various stages of the project, and particularly to Neil Paynter who worked through the typescript in painstaking detail and improved it in countless small but significant ways. Most of all, we owe a particular debt of gratitude to the six other friends who shared that original Christmas with us at Cropthorne, out of which this book was born – and also to Peter Middlemass, the warden of Holland House, Cropthorne, who trusted us with free rein of the house and offered it to us at a ludicrously modest rent. Peter Kettle has been particularly closely involved in the evolution of this project, undertaking the time-consuming survey research in the congregations mentioned above, reading through many of the submissions with us and offering constructive critical comments at various stages of our work. We gladly dedicate this book to him and to the other friends who made up the original 'Cropthorne eight'. Our hope is that it will inspire many more 'alternative Christmases' to come.

Nicola Slee and Rosie Miles,
Stirchley,
April 2006

Part One

Personal Stories and Reflections

Chapter One

Family Christmases

One of the media fantasies of Christmas, perpetuated by TV adverts, glossy magazine articles and such like, is that it is a time of unremitting domestic bliss and family togetherness. Images of happy families gathered round the fire or the groaning festive table abound. Whilst many people *do* enjoy time with family over the Christmas period, the reality for most of us is far more ambivalent than the fantasy allows. Even if we love our families and get on with them, many of us live in complicated, extended or fragmented family networks, with multiple and diverse groupings to relate to, often geographically dispersed, and this puts a strain on resources and energy – at a time of the year when travel is most fraught. And then for many of us, relationships with family are complex and difficult, adding to the pressures and tensions. We may prefer to spend the festival with friends or with 'adopted' family, going against the grain of cultural expectations. Ironically, it may be when we are away from family that we can most readily admit our connection to them and give thanks for them.

The pieces in this chapter explore different versions of family Christmases. They are truthful about the ambiguities and tensions of family gatherings – the silences, the losses, the boredom, the conflicts. A few are unremittingly cynical or sober, reminding us that Christmas is the time of year when the household is under the greatest strain and when incidences of domestic violence and murder are at their height. Others suggest ways of spending Christmas with family in ways that cut across the prevailing norms and include the outsider.

Some joy to all!

I hate Christmas. I don't see why people gush about how great it is – and what's all this crap about a white Christmas? Either people love freezing to death or it's a race thing. It's amazing how they forget all the accidents caused by snow even when the idiot drivers are sober and not speeding. All the people stranded at their offices or trapped in their homes, the frozen pipes, the icy roads, people taking twelve hours to do a one-hour journey, all the old people who are found dead at home – how come it always takes weeks to find them, even when they do have families?

And don't get me started on family get-togethers! People who hate each other are not gonna stop just for one day because it's Christmas. If anything, putting people and booze into a tight environment will definitely cause wholesale slaughter. I heard on the radio one time that a man took a carving knife to his wife because she complained about the way he was cutting up the turkey. And you're always hearing about people doing dumb things at Christmas parties because of too much booze. I heard that the suicide rate goes up at Christmas. Ha! Some joy to all! Me, I don't put up decorations or a tree. I never had a good time at Christmas and now that I'm on my own it hasn't changed much. And I hate visiting people; they always get to going on about how 'much' they've done the whole year. Families always know where to dig in the knife.

I don't buy presents; I might go round the sales if I have any money – I'm unemployed so I'll see. What's the point anyway? Buying stuff you can't afford and probably will only just have paid for by the next Christmas, and the people and kids don't like it or break it before Boxing Day, if they're not sick or drunk or if they're still talking to you, which you probably don't want them to, and all the old family grudges always come out.

'E'

A grandparent's reflection

Even for those with families, celebrating Christmas isn't an unmitigated idyll. The vexed question: 'Which of our parents are we going to spend Christmas with?' can be a bone of contention between husband and wife in many marriages. Even grandparents can be faced with difficult choices, the best solutions perhaps involving long journeys at a difficult time of year.

Personally I would always be happier to spend Christmas at home, with the families of both our daughter and our son coming to us, but I know that it may be more difficult for them to travel, with the children becoming increasingly vocal about wanting to spend time with their local friends, and the various commitments such as our son-in-law playing the organ at church on Christmas Day – not to mention the equal rights of the other grandparents, living as far north as we do south, to be visited during the holiday season. I could almost be envious of friends without grandchildren who can choose where they want to spend the festival – except that I do really want to see my grandchildren opening their presents.

And that raises the real problem: what to give children who have it all, whose parents will probably be spending far more on them than we think they should, or than we spent on our own children when they were young?! Grandchildren who will rip the paper off in seconds, forget what they've been given or indicate that they already have it, and who seem to find the most interesting aspect to be whether they have accumulated more money in presents than their siblings.

Many years ago, when our own children were young, we invited two foreign students to come to stay with us at Christmas. The charity through which we did this sent us two men, one from Poland and one from Japan; the latter in particular was very keen to do everything that was appropriate to an English Christmas.

Those without immediate family responsibilities have a greater scope for doing Christmas differently, which may provide interesting opportunities. Though I'm happy to spend Christmas with the family, it would be inaccurate to conjure up a beatific vision of a placid grandmother surrounded by worshipping grandchildren!

Pat Pinsent

Childless at Christmas

Joseph is the person with whom I feel a particular affinity at Christmas. I feel an affinity with this man because he does not really have a role to play in the Christmas narrative: Jesus is not his child and yet he is expected to enter into the celebrations as if he was the birth father. If Christmas is all about children – and this is something I have heard on many occasions – I, like Joseph, find myself strangely outside it. I have yearned for children, but they have never arrived. This does not mean that I am reluctant to celebrate the coming of Christ, but simply that an emphasis on the birth of a baby leaves me with whispers of what might have been rather than with something that I can truly participate in.

Christmas carols about a newborn king or a baby sleeping gently on golden hay leave me standing at the door of the Christmas festivities, watching but not really feeling invited to join in. I hope this does not make me sound like Uncle Ebenezer; indeed, I delighted in my nephew's first Christmas and first Boxing Day pantomime. Nor, as an Anglican priest, am I, through my childlessness, unable to share in the delight of a child showing off his or her toy at the Christmas morning service, or in the excitement of the new bike been ridden through the estate. Nevertheless, as I witness such sights, my heart weeps for the children left outside, those who have nothing for Christmas except the prospect of further broken dreams. Perhaps my childlessness gives me a particular empathy for children who are left outside in the cold at Christmas. Thank God for the growing number of Christingle services in support of the work done daily by The Children's Society.

It is not all the parties, food and drink that leave me feeling a little lost in the annual festivities. In truth, I enjoy the occasional visit from friends, as well as an invitation for my wife, Jennifer, and me to be part of a larger family group. Rather, what disenfranchises me from Christmas is what the story itself has become. Christmas in the UK is no longer about light invading the darkness or hope overcoming fear – as witnessed in the lives of men and women like Joseph and Mary, Zechariah and Elizabeth (another unusual birth), the shepherds and the Magi. It is not about the coming of one who included all, even those whom we struggle to look directly in the eye. The Christmas story 21st-century style, for churchgoer and non-churchgoer alike, has been reduced to the sweet lullaby of the Virgin Mother to a contented baby. It is non-threatening and detached from the reality of those of us who have struggled with fertility tests and the non-advent of a long-hoped-for child. Possibly it is also detached from the reality of parents whose children are irrepressibly more human than the baby depicted asleep in a food trough. The childless do not have a monopoly on feeling uncomfortable with Christmas.

So what do I do about it? I could say that I strip away the story from its sanitised version, releasing Jesus to be the light of the world, rather than a little person trapped in swaddling bands. But that would be a lie that would come back to haunt me. I might like to say that I just enter into the spirit of what is on offer, but I had better not in case someone who knows me is reading this. And, just occasionally, I might feel like stamping my feet and clenching my fists at the season to be jolly, and crying out: 'Bah! Humbug!' to it all.

What I do most of the time, however, is to attempt to hold together both the enjoyment of a festival centred on a child and the pain of childlessness – as impossible as that seems sometimes – and to try to ensure that my Christmas disenfranchises no one. I laugh and cry, eat and drink, keep company with friends as well as spending time just with Jennifer – and try to remember that for one day it is OK to feel an affinity with Joseph.

Kevin Ellis

To everything a season

Christmas 1990 was my first without my mother, Lou. She died six months before that on June 5th. A year earlier she had spent Christmas with us – my father, sister, husband, mum-in-law and two children, whom she adored, always spoiling them with too many presents. We guessed at that time that this would probably be her last Christmas, and she also feared it, although she did not speak of it directly. Boxing Day was her birthday and I have clear memories of her making pastry for the apple pie for the celebratory lunch and of her saying grace for us, praying for the blessing of God on our meal and on our lives.

Christmas Days had always followed a fairly set pattern and in 1990 we decided to try to do things as usual. This involved us in a game of pretending that everything was OK. We invited a friend who, significantly, had never met my mother to share the day with us. Unconsciously, I guess we were trying to build protection against facing our feelings and each other. I remember it as a day when I was aware of forcing myself to keep going and to get to the end no matter what. But throughout the day I felt the churning fear that is often part of the early days of mourning. At certain points in the day the sadness was heavy and tangible – but we carried on. Only my father had the grace to weep when it came to giving presents to the children.

I wish we could have spoken our loss: that we could have found a language to give voice to the depth of our feelings. What we needed was a ritual space in which to name her, to honour together her very real presence amongst us. Much is written of the need for the bereaved to 'let go' of their dead. Christmas family gatherings may need rituals that help us to receive them back. The following poem reflects both how it was and a longing for how it might have been.

For Lou

It was a time for mourning
but instead we danced.
Out of step with the heavy beat of our hearts,
we feigned a lightness of foot.
But the tune of our memories grew loud and strong,
beckoning us to stop and name you;
to allow you to lead us in the slow rhythmic movements
of grief outpoured.

It was a time for weeping
but instead we laughed.
Hollow nonsense filled the air
We smiled the smiles of fools.
But the river of your presence burst the banks of our folly

and flowed through us,
summoning us to bathe our wounds
in the cleansing tears
of absence named.

It was a time for silence
but we spoke.
On and on, straining to fill the spaces.
But your whispered song of stillness
caressed our discordant words,
teaching us to wait,
to be still and listen.
To know you
lovingly with us.

Christine Worsley

Home for Christmas

He wakes up crying.
It seems a little obscene,
lying in the guest room
on this freezing Friday morning.

It's a double – twin divan,
littered with this season's crop
of index-linked accessories:
the whistling key ring, the Filofax frog.

What more could a grown man ask for?
A cuddle with the landlady?
A visit from the guy in red?
A pillow fight with a *Star Wars* duvet?

And he wonders what he's doing,
crying in the guest room
on this freezing Friday morning.

Helen Buckingham

Far from home

On the table cold tongue pants under fairy lights
and mince pies suffocate in sugar.
Beneath the telly sausage rolls sweat in Tupperware
while we scramble between legs and chairs and farts
to look up Auntie Sheila's skirt.
We knock back the dregs of Drambuie, Advocaat and beer,
drunk on a Christmas cheer
that's eighty miles south
and buried deeper than bone.

Gail Ashton

Santa's bicycle

We stuck Santa up with Blu-Tack.
There he sat, illuminated,
pedalling uphill in our window,
wheels flashing.

It was not until we went outside
we realised he was back to front.

That Christmas came unwrapped.
There were empty chairs.
We didn't bother with pudding.
Later it rained,
spiteful lashes against the window.

But nothing deterred Santa.
He kept on regardless,
pedalling backwards.

Liz Verlander

The day before Christmas Eve

Cradled in the sofa's arms
as the darkness settles in
on this shortest of days

reading a new book
eating satsumas –
their skins unfolding like golden stars
the sweet-sharp pungent scent
drifting among the smoky winter potpourri
the sound of the radio from the kitchen
the rustle of present-wrapping
from the next room.

We have come through together –
closer, though a little scarred –
and created this sense of peace:
fragrant, fragile, transient.

This is the moment of silence
at the top of the wave:
before the phone rings
before the train arrives
before the door is opened
before the barbarian hordes
before the thunder rolls ...

Christine Vial

Christmas at Auntie Ray's

I was brought up by a very sociable great-aunt. My mother died when I was seven years old; my father remarried but was never able or willing to provide a permanent home for me and my brother. So there I was, in the loving care of an aunt fifty years my senior, who had dwindling resources (this was wartime) but an infinite capacity to draw people into her hospitable home. Christmas at Aunty Ray's place was a constant coming and going. We always fitted in morning service at our local Anglican church, but from then onwards it was sherry, gin and tonic, and whisky and soda with friends and neighbours, followed by a splendid dinner with all the trimmings and exhaustion in front of the fire. By evening we had got out the card table and were hard at it: rummy, vingt-et-un, draughts, Monopoly, and snap for any little cousins or spare children.

When I had my own family, I must have unconsciously remembered those Christmases with everyone swept in to enjoy the fun around the tree, the presents, the crackers, the games, the decorations and that mysterious excitement that always accompanied the festivities. To begin with, we used to invite lonely overseas students from our local polytechnic to spend the day with us. It was heart-warming to see how their initial shyness soon melted away as the children drew them into the family circle. Several years later, I was widowed; then, in addition to my four young children, I had an extended family: a Rwandan student, soon to be joined by his sister and brother. I quickly learned that when you take Rwandans to your heart, you take on an indefinite number of their relations and friends as well. 'Mother, could I invite a couple we know for Christmas? They're on their own.' 'Yes, of course, Geoffrey.' 'Actually, Mother, they have three children.' 'A bit of a squash at bedtime, Geoffrey?' 'Not a problem: they can all share a room.' Being together with loving friends was what was important, not a bedroom each and an en-suite bathroom. Food, fun and fellowship, says the grace before meals. How much we all learned from our Rwandan family!

We used to all troop down to morning service and cause quite a sensation: my adopted daughter is Vietnamese, one son's wife is Swedish, another's is half-Japanese, another's is Zulu, Geoffrey's is Burundian; the children, of course, reflect the ethnic identities of their parents. With our Rwandan extended family, we multiplied the ethnic and cultural diversity of the congregation at Winchester Cathedral considerably. Back home, as I looked round the Christmas lunch table or listened to the chatter around the kitchen sink, the message proclaimed by the angels – 'Peace on Earth, goodwill to all!' – seemed to hover over us.

Our traditional Christmas has always been enriched by the presence of friends and strangers, sharing the gifts that the astonishing birth in Bethlehem offers to us all. Now my adult children have taken over the rituals of Christmas. And I am deeply thankful that this pattern of real hospitality and welcome is still alive in them

– far more important than the size of the turkey or the number of presents around the tree.

Elizabeth Salter

The Christmas cassette

The cassette sat in my hand. I was afraid to put it in my Walkman but knew that I must. It was Christmas Day and this was a link with home. The spools and ribbon would be worthless to anyone else. On it I knew would be sentiments of love, pauses of regret and clutches of anxiety meant only for me, the eldest child, the unlikely prodigal.

I sighed and looked around: a veranda next to the hostel pool with views of Table Mountain – not quite what I expected when I signed up for Voluntary Service Overseas. I had come with mission book images of hardship and sacrifice, of being freed from the burdens of Western wealth and doing a desert mother impression in the Namibian sand. (Fortunately my dream was not the reality.) Much to my disappointment my house at the school had both water and electricity, and I had still not learnt how to slaughter a chicken. Now, like most of the other volunteers, I had chosen to escape the desert heat, ignore the ripples of guilt in my soul that reminded me of my relative affluence, and head to the Cape Town coast to cool off for Christmas.

As I sat on the veranda, I was conscious of feeling lucky. I'd been able to follow a dream, and now, this Christmas Day, I revelled in the sense of freedom, but loathed the feeling of rootlessness. My temporary residence in the backpackers' hostel embodied both. I was missing home, but scared of what I might hear. Reluctantly, I reconnected with my family. The cassette was a gift from my dad on the day I left, marked in block capitals: FOR CHRISTMAS DAY ONLY. His voice started: 'Hiya Karen. If you are listening to this it must be Christmas Day, and that means that it will be the first Christmas Day that you haven't been with us since you were born.' The tears streamed down my face as he talked to me. Awful jokes interspersed with Christmas songs and reassurances that I was missed. Then came the voice of my mum. I heard the note of false jollity underlined by fear. Her little girl was in Africa, a long way from home. 'I always said we should never have let you read all those Enid Blyton stories, it filled your head with ideas of adventures.' Adventures aren't something you are supposed to have if you have grown up in my home town; a council house near your mum is more the norm. I had let her down.

My mind drifted back to other Christmases. The tempers and tears. Presents offered and rejected. The feelings of dysfunctional family failure. But just before the chaos began – the midnight service. 'The peace of the Lord be always with you.' Then the return from church, to be met by my sister just home from the pub. Now for our sacred space. A drink together: a yearly ritual of communion, repentance and exhortation, carried without any formal liturgy but underwritten by love. It was our only contact in the year. My sister and I are not close, but over time this hour on Christmas Eve had come to be significant. It was an affirmation of a relationship that transcended sibling rivalry and the physical distance that we had each put between home and ourselves. On Christmas Eve I had come to receive communion of two kinds: balm that would soothe the emotional bruises to come. Pain would follow on Christmas Day, the sort of cruelty that can only be inflicted effectively by those who know you best. Achilles' heels cannot be kept secret in families; you each know the weaknesses of the other, there to exploit at times of stress.

Sat in Cape Town I was surprised to note that I missed my family. Strange how something that can cause so much pain can also be a source of such love. I had thought that I wanted to get away from them, but somehow this felt too far. Perhaps it was a rejection of them, but if it was then it was also a rejection of part of me. And that was something that I could not run away from. I was and am built from those parts, shaped by mother, father and sister. Whatever experiences might be added, however I tried to remould myself, I could not undermine that foundation, and so the grief flowed.

Other travellers glanced at me quizzically as they passed, but let me be. They too carried some sadness. For one middle-aged couple it was the death of their teenage daughter – they wanted to be surrounded by youth. For another woman it was the thoughts of her husband eating turkey without her; for one young man some tears glistened for his girlfriend. Later we would party, celebrate our independence and break from cloying family routines. There would be a lightness and joy. But first we had to mourn. For the illusions of independence and freedom are costly and each must pay according to their means.

Tears spent, I returned the cassette to its case.

Karen Jobson

Let the bells jingle

Let the bells jingle but make time for the tears to fall.
Eat, drink and be merry but do not go hungry in that inner place.
Rest, reflect and remember. Be true to yourself.
Many of us can't play happy families at this time of the year.

December is for a difficult diagnosis as well as dreaming of a white Christmas.
December is for divorce as well as decorations.
December is for death and dying as well as discos and dancing.
December is for distances that separate us from people,
        even those in the same room.

Disappointments in December are especially hard to bear.
Sometimes the light no longer shines in the darkness.
The desolation swallows us up and we die a little.

Yet a kindly word, a bird in flight, a tree alive with hoar and hips
can drown out despair and kindle determination to move on.
Dig down deeper than the tinsel to the place where hope is found.
Maybe, just maybe, the flickering flame will be fanned gently into fire.

Helen Jesty

Chapter Two
Alternative Community Christmases

Not everyone can, or wants to, spend Christmas with their blood relatives: family members may be separated by thousands of miles or may be unwelcoming or too difficult to choose to be with! Or, if we do spend Christmas with family, it may be that, paradoxically, we experience real community elsewhere – in passing encounters with neighbours or precisely when the family is widened to include others beyond blood ties. In this chapter, we consider stories of alternative community settings: informal gatherings of neighbours, deliberate attempts to create alternative community (such as the Cropthorne gathering from which this book had its genesis) and going to stay with a religious community over Christmas. Not that these attempts to create or join with alternative communities are complete panaceas in themselves: they may solve some problems but create new ones. Alternative communities can be fragile and fleeting spaces in which to encounter authentic communion; and, indeed, the friend or stranger may be as difficult to live with as one's own family members. Nevertheless, because there is still very heavy pressure to see Christmas as 'family time', and often heavy pressure to spend the festival with one's blood relatives, any attempt to do something different seems worth noting and celebrating.

Christmas – a priest's progress

The bottom dropped out of family Christmas with grandma's death in my mid-teens. Everyone – her four daughters, their husbands and seven grandchildren – had gathered at the grandparents in the 1950s and early '60s for Christmas Day tea (tinned salmon, celery, trifle, Christmas cake …) and for the rest of the evening, some trying to watch *Christmas Night With The Stars* on a rather ropey early television set. But after she died, extended family life fragmented – no more so than at Christmas, when it seemed as though we all retreated into our own small family units.

And then my mother never liked cooking. There was a flip side to a Bing Crosby Christmas record in those days which asked: 'Why can't we have Christmas the whole year round?' To which we answered in chorus: 'Because mam wouldn't be able to do the cooking.'

Undergraduate years passed under the above dispensation, ordination providing the perfect opportunity not to go home for Christmas (and, 28 years later, I have not slept over at 'home' for any of them). In my early years as a curate, a friend and I quietly enjoyed an annual feast of not quite normal Christmas fare – a roast hand of pork and college pudding – and had to go along to slightly hearty vicarage parties. In my years as a vicar in the early 1980s, there was more than one Christmas gathering in the vicarage of those who couldn't – or didn't want to – go back home for the ritual visit. But in those years other questions emerged for me, partly by way of comparing and contrasting Christmas and Easter. To start with, at least with Easter you know where you are with days of the week (even if the *date* is not fixed). For Christians at least, our weekly cycle of 'work, rest and pray' is thrown into confusion by 'the moveable feast' that falls on December 25th. At Easter, although there is a sense of anticlimax afterwards, it is nothing like as bad as the crash after what has become, in many places, a damp squib of a Christmas morning service following the 'high' point of midnight mass. At least at Easter, the days are lengthening and the following week is more of an opportunity to quietly savour the resurrection, rather than collapse into somnolent exhaustion.

And what have we been celebrating? It seems to me that it is becoming increasingly difficult to celebrate the incarnation through the biblical narratives, which have become, through the medium of 'nativity plays' and the like, more akin to fairy stories. In some places the 'crib service' is becoming a real attraction for *adults*; and its timing (along with the broadcast of the *Festival of Nine Lessons* and *Carols from King's College, Cambridge*) on the afternoon of Christmas Eve helps to get religious observation and duty out of the way as early as possible.

Over nineteen years since leaving full-time ministry, I have either worked or been on call for nine of them, precluding either committing myself to taking church services or drinking too much! On a further six occasions I have been abroad, where Christmas is taken rather more reasonably than in the UK.

The high point of experimentation with Christmas (it seems to me that this is not generally felt to be a season for trying out radical new ideas) was planning and executing, with Nicola Slee, a residential Christmas away, following an 'alternative' Holy Week and Easter a few years before. Both events were planned to explore creative, alternative seasonal liturgies, self-cater in a simple, wholesome way and explore living in community through the seasonal experience. While the Easter event had been open to all comers, we decided to restrict the Christmas experiment to a group of invited friends. We were, I think, rightly anxious about the effects of 'doing Christmas differently', especially on any who had never done it differently at all.

In fact, only one of the eight participants came without a sense of complete exhaustion, because of the pressures of the season, personal problems or recent traumatic events. Settling into living together, let alone working on alternative Christmas celebrations, was hard and at times tearful. I believe our liturgies (included in this book) were enormously helpful in resolving the problems. So was the setting – a glorious retreat house in the Midlands, with lots of space (and spaces) and beautiful grounds. Tears turned to laughter – and I do not expect to have a better Christmas evening than I had that year, sitting around the television, watching the *French and Saunders Christmas Special* as one man in the company of seven women.

That was six years ago, and I have not – so far – wanted to try another one; if nothing else, it took some time to recover! Since then I have, for various reasons, begun to relate to Anglican parish life more closely than at any time since I resigned as a vicar in 1985. And yet so far I have kept away from Christmas in church, sometimes still choosing to go abroad. Liturgically, the season feels somehow detached from the main run of parochial worship, with the social upheavals of people going away and visitors attending an unfamiliar church with probably very different expectations. To minister liturgically at Christmas still feels – and perhaps always has been – uncomfortable.

Peter Kettle

Christmas with neighbours

Some of the best Christmases I've had were spent with my immediate neighbours. Like the year I was in panto in Liverpool and couldn't get home between performances. We did a show on Christmas Eve and two on Boxing Day, and on Christmas Day joined a large party at one of the theatre houses. It was great fun and there was no emotional blackmail involved. However, my mother never forgave me for 'not going home' and brought the event up every year until she died!

We get on well with our neighbours here in Carlton; we are families, couples and single people who always join together for something at Christmas – Christmas Eve dinner, a breakfast on Boxing Day. Nobody need feel left out and nobody is forced to come. I realise this is unusual these days when people quite often don't know their neighbours.

In my brother's parish, the church joins up with the local care home for Christmas dinner in the village hall and sundry aunts and in-laws have to join in or not come! My late father actually enjoyed this more then he used to let on – far more than the 'family' Christmas meal when my mum was alive, which I remember as always being fraught with tensions and people getting prickly and defensive with one another.

Rowena Edlin-White

Pastrami on rye

I used to love going over to Syd and Meg's on Christmas Day. Frankie and I would slip over there soon (but not too soon) after everyone at our parents' had slowly opened their presents. Although we had an eight-foot-tall artificial tree, a ceramic nativity set a great-grandmother had carefully handed down, and the house was redolent with the scent of spruce – boughs festooned polished banisters – Christmas Day at my parents' house didn't really feel festive. My father would sit in his easy chair trying to watch football over the Mormon Tabernacle Choir on the phonograph, and jump, not whenever his side scored but every time my mother suddenly called out to him from the kitchen for some reason. So, it was either pretend to still like football with my depressed father, or watch my manic mother cook up a storm. Or wander back and forth between the two.

'Ho! Ho! Ho!' was how Syd would resoundingly greet us, wearing his Santa suit and holding his jiggling sides. He'd give us both a mighty, heartfelt, bone-crushing hug then strip us of our heavy coats. Elfin Meg would give us a beer and an affectionate peck we had to stoop for. Then Syd would come back and ask Frankie if he'd like to sample a nibble of what he gave his reindeer to fly. Then, right in front of his daughter, Shelly, and me, he'd expertly roll and strike up a doobie. 'She'd find out sooner or later,' shrugged Meg, waiting for them to pass it round. 'Ya, we don't wanna keep secrets from her,' rasped Syd, holding in a healthy toke. I don't think Shelly, who was around 13 or 14, was allowed to partake yet, but I was welcome to come sit in the circle if I wanted. I always politely declined though. Frankie counselled me to say no to drugs, and I saw that it made him proud when I said no thank you.

Soon we'd move the party into the living room. There were no plastic-protected sofas and armchairs no one ever sat in here, just a big, worn, cushy black couch pushed back against a bare wall, and a long, low chrome and glass table. In the centre of the table sat a big ceramic ashtray. The table was ringed all over from beer cans. In the ashtray was probably about enough evidence to put Syd away for a year or more.

Even if Syd and Meg had wanted more furniture and things in their living room, not much else would have fit. Syd's stereo, which was the reason we'd all moved in there in the first place, was awesome. Black, six-and-a-half-foot-high speakers he'd got a deal on from some disco that had – thank God – gone out of business. Syd had one of the best turntables and tuners money could buy. Both made by some obscure Japanese company with a name that, after a couple of beers, was impossible to properly pronounce, and which manufactured, Syd said, only a few thousand units a year. His graphic equaliser was very Christmassy, blinking little red and green lights that danced merrily to the joyous music. Syd would put on cut after rockin' cut, pristine album after album, but couldn't edge the volume over three or four or he'd risk putting more cracks in his ceiling and disturbing his easy-listening neighbours.

While Syd would be busily playing DJ, Meg would bring us another tall can of Miller High Life and maybe some cold cuts and crumbly old cheddar cheese on a silver tray. I'd sneak a glance at Shelly from time to time. Tall, lithe Shelly was two full years younger than me but looked around 20, and acted older than anyone in the room. Changing albums, Syd remarked that she wanted to be a fashion model when she grew up. 'Don't cha Shell?' 'Yes, dad,' she responded with a roll of her chocolate eyes and a bothered sigh. 'Rented her an elf suit too but she wouldn't wear it.'

There was enough space for Shelly to come join her folks on the couch, but she instead chose a wooden-backed chair she'd dragged in from the kitchen. (I was cross-legged on the green shag.) As if practising a pose, Shelly sat staring straight ahead, her sheer stockinged legs crossed, and swaying when she forgot herself. I was glad the music was loud and that I didn't have to try to make conversation.

Frankie and I would spend Christmas Day at Syd and Meg's free and easy. We'd dance round megalithic speakers, eat, drink and be merry. 'Merry Christmas! Rock 'n' roll!' We all sat in silence a minute for saints who had died: for Janis and Morrison and Jimi

They'd always ask us to stay for supper. It was always going to be something simple, like pastrami on rye. 'With some of that Keen's hot mustard. Ooo wee, that's good stuff! Really clears out the sinuses.' 'We'd love to but can't.' 'We gotta be back.' They'd understand. And we'd slowly put our heavy coats back on. 'Give your mom and dad our love,' they'd call out into the cold night, standing in the doorway, wrapped in a warm aura.

Man, just unreal, the smell that rushed up to greet you when you walked in the door of my parents' place at dinnertime on a holiday, or on most any Sunday afternoon for that matter. So homey and healthy. Like falling into the pages of *Better Homes and Gardens*. For Christmas dinner my mother would cook a twenty-pound goose stuffed with wild rice and chestnuts, baby potatoes, brussels sprout purée with toasted cashews, green beans with lemon butter, pearl onions in a crème sauce, glazed yams, spinach sprinkled with grated nutmeg … She'd top it all off with a Christmas pudding à la Dickens, which she'd serve with a flourish of her long-fingered hand and flaming brandy.

And while my charming brother would say that everything was excellent – 'just excellent. Excellento!' – I'd sit silently at the long, antique table in the jumpy, nervous light of tall red candles in faceted brass holders, feeling disdainful and guilty, and wishing I was back at Syd and Meg's savouring pastrami and dill pickles.

'Spoiled your dinner with a lot of junk, didn't you?'

Forks scraped, knives clashed. Crystal chimed. Dark looks shimmered and brimmed in my father's and mother's eyes, and around the dinner table everything unsaid broke free, and hung and drifted and swirled.

Nick Waters

A boatload of friends

We were living on an old wooden boat that was threatening to sink under us. The kitchen was tiny and the head height, 5′3″. That was okay for us – both Ros and I are 5′2″. How did we end up hosting eleven people for Christmas dinner in a living space barely 10′ x 10′?

As boat-dwellers we had far more space then conventional narrow boats, our living area being half as wide again as the standard. Parties that started life on the towpath often ended up onboard. Our friends either seemed to have no relatives, or no relatives they could contemplate spending time with. Boat-dwelling does not attract people who enjoy a close family life. Christmas seemed to be a lonely time that was difficult to get through. Ros and I enjoy hospitality, and so we decided we would invite any who cared to come for a Christmas Day meal.

Ros had relatives nearby so we arranged to meet them for coffee on Christmas morning before rushing back to the boat; we were also to spend Boxing Day with them. My youngest son lived close to the mooring and was still single so he was invited to the Christmas meal.

Going out in the morning meant that we couldn't cook the meat. Our oven was not reliable enough to leave unattended and in any case was too small to fit much in. As the number of guests grew we realised that we would need to share out the food preparation. A house-dwelling friend with a full-size cooker was given the job of cooking the turkey. Luckily, she also had a car to transport it. We decided to do the roast potatoes and the sprouts, as the timing was critical for them. Other friends offered to provide various vegetables, sauces, gravy, custard and so on, according to their kitchens, budgets or cooking abilities. Everyone was to bring his or her own plate, bowl, cutlery, mug and alcohol.

As zero hour approached guests began to arrive, saucepans in hand. Some sauntered in with pans of vegetables needing to be reheated. Others appeared out of breath, the sauce still bubbling. The woodstove made it warm, almost uncomfortably so, as we crushed into the smoky fug. Somehow order was created and we sat down, mostly on the floor, to tuck in. Nearby, boaters had left the puddings steaming whilst we all ate the first course.

There is nothing like trying to step over people with a pan of carrots in your hand to encourage introductions – especially on a boat that could lurch suddenly as another guest climbed the gangplank. Amazingly, the meal worked remarkably well. As a bonus for us, everyone took home their own washing-up, and we divided up the few leftovers between us so that no one was overwhelmed.

I had been dubious about inviting one friend. Not only was he 6'6" tall, but also had severe mental health problems. The thought of Andy 'freaking out' in such a confined space was daunting. He was confident he would cope, but I remained worried. Some of those coming knew him, and would try to give him the space he needed. Others would be meeting him for the first time. Eventually, I decided that it would be unfair to exclude him on the basis of what *might* happen. Anything was possible: I could scald a guest with hot water, someone could fall into the canal … I could think of numerous dire scenarios if I let myself. In the event, Andy managed the meal but left hurriedly without saying goodbye as soon as he had popped the last fragment into his mouth. That was progress: he had shown he knew himself well enough to know when things were getting too much for him. I was so glad he had come and had not spent the entire day alone.

It might have been Christmas, but presents were banned. Not everyone knew each other. Some, the friend with the house and car, for example, earned good money. Most of us were struggling with our finances. Ros worked part-time and I was a student. Some were on benefits or had taken early retirement. One couple seemed to subsist on thin air, having 'dropped out' of the system completely. Anyhow, boaters don't usually have enough room for all the things they've already got, without adding to the clutter. Those who wanted to exchange gifts did so either before or after the event.

Despite the overcrowding and the lack of seats, most people seemed in no hurry to leave. Some had to go on to visit family, and left reluctantly. The rest of us settled back. We had not had to put on a display, provide expensive presents or elaborate food. Instead, we had all shared our resources in order to help one another enjoy the day. It felt good.

Ruth Farrer

Abbey Christmas

For a good number of years in my twenties and thirties – perhaps a dozen – I spent almost every Christmas at St Mary's Abbey, West Malling, the home of an enclosed Benedictine community of Anglican nuns. Although my wider family usually got together in various groupings before or after Christmas, by tacit agreement we all did our own thing at Christmas. Occasionally I broke the pattern of my abbey Christmases – I spent one Christmas with a friend and her family; another time I went to Bruges with a different friend – but the times at the Abbey were the norm.

I had originally been introduced to Malling Abbey when living in London, and immediately felt myself deeply drawn by its austere and ancient beauty, its simplicity, its stability and the commitment of the nuns to a hidden life of prayer. Sheltered behind high walls and nestling amongst apple orchards, with a little stream running through its gardens, the Abbey consists of a cluster of buildings, the oldest going back to the 12th and 14th centuries, at the centre of which stands the huge 1960s' concrete church in which the nuns sing their seven-fold office day in, day out, starting with Vigils at 4.30 am and ending with Compline at 7.30 pm. Around this basic framework, their pattern of life consists of a balanced routine of manual work, study, private prayer and recreation. As in all Benedictine communities, guests are received with simple and loving hospitality, welcomed 'as Christ' into the midst of the community to share its life of prayer and worship and to draw on the silence and beauty of the place.

One of the things I most value about the hospitality offered by religious communities (and I have experienced this in other places too) is the way that it combines both genuine warmth and welcome with a radical respect for the freedom and solitude of the guest. Those who come are welcomed into the community for a number of days or weeks, and few, if any, questions are asked about background, job, status or belief. There is no fixed charge, people being invited to give what they can afford according to conscience. Guests are welcome to attend chapel but there is no requirement to do so. Beyond accepting the rules of the house in terms of mealtimes and the keeping of silence at certain hours, there is a huge freedom for the individual to use their time as they wish. The sisters are present and available to talk to when needed, and other guests are generally friendly (some can be talkative!) but for much of the time one is left alone with one's own thoughts and solitude, free to wander about the grounds, to read, to sleep, to rest, to pray. Underlying this is a fundamental trust on the part of the sisters in God as Host, the one who draws guests and meets with them, ministering to them in and through the life and witness of the community. This combination of strong holding provided by a community of prayer with the setting free of the guest to be alone with themselves and with God seems to me one of the unique gifts of religious communities in our time, and one which vast numbers of people respond to hungrily from both within and outside the boundaries of the church.

At any time of year, this experience of hospitality in a place of great beauty and deeply lived prayer is a powerful one. At Christmas, it has been, for me, immensely healing and liberating. By the time I arrive at the Abbey gates towards the end of December, I am usually completely exhausted by the intensity of the teaching term, the usual round of parties, social events and carol services and all the hectic Christmas preparations. There is a profound relief at being able to sink into the silence and darkness of the winter rhythm of this place where I am known and loved – and let be. In the space I can recover from the madness of the pre-Christmas build-up, gather my thoughts and sift my emotions, give my body and mind the rest they desperately crave. Paradoxically, in the silence and solitude I am able to become more aware of all the many people with whom my life is connected. I always take my cards with me and stick them up on the wooden beams that run the length of my room in the 14th-century guesthouse, and give time to re-reading the messages and thinking about all the people from whom I have chosen to be physically absent at this time yet come close to in my thoughts and prayer.

The guesthouse is usually full for Christmas itself. Many who would otherwise be alone come to this place where they are welcomed in and can form community. A good number of the guests are elderly women, some of them related to the nuns or long-term friends; but there are usually a few younger guests as well. We are a temporary community of oddbods – spinsters, widows, singles, misfits and solitaries of one kind or another – drawn here for a motley collection of reasons. We may have little in common with each other beyond our connection to the Abbey, yet, over the few days we are together (and, in some cases, over the years that we re-gather), we form a fragile and fleeting community. Oddly, it may be easier to be with strangers at

this time of year than with one's own kith and kin; somehow I can extend to these
fellow guests the gentleness and reverence I may struggle to offer to my own family.
I am conscious of the irony of that, and know my own frailty. I think of my family as
I dip into the chocolates or swop stories with these transitory fellow pilgrims, and
ask forgiveness that I am here, rather than with them.

The rhythm and routine of the Benedictine day holds me firmly and securely at a
time of year when my body is deeply tired and my emotions are usually pretty near
the surface. Indeed, the space allows painful feelings and memories of past Christmases to surface; at some point, I have learnt, there will be tears and feelings of loneliness and longing, sometimes quite acute. Yet I am safe here to allow them to be and
to give them room, in a way that might not be so elsewhere.

In the spirit of Benedictine simplicity and reverence for material things, the celebrations for Christmas are modest and yet have a power and beauty that can take my
breath away. The liturgy is at the heart of life here, now and at every season of the
year. The sombre cadences and rich scriptural images of Advent are given full sway
in the sweep and rhythm of the daily offices. There is a sense of building up to the
drama and climax of the incarnation, which becomes particularly intense towards
the end of Advent when the 'O' antiphons appear at Vespers and human longing and
anticipation is at its keenest. Advent is allowed to take its full course, and decorations do not appear in the guesthouse until Christmas Eve – and when they do, they
are of the simplest kind: a single bare branch placed in a pot, with paper decorations
attached to the twigs; a few pots of winter jasmine and greenery in the refectory; the
sisters' own printed cards and, sometimes, a booklet, appearing outside one's door
on Christmas Eve. Somehow, these naïve gestures of restrained festivity have a far
greater impact than any number of sophisticated and opulent designer decorations
one can buy on the high street.

When we get to Christmas itself, the day is marked by many small and joyful
touches: special fruit bread and bananas at breakfast, a full traditional dinner at
which guests are free to talk over the meal (the only time, apart from Easter, when
this happens), a visit to the guesthouse of the mother abbess after dinner when we
listen to the Queen's Speech and enjoy more conversation. There may be visits – or
'parlours', as they are called – to meet with the one or two nuns with whom one has
formed particular friendships over the years. And of course, the Christmas liturgy
marks the change of mood from the minor tones of Advent to the wonder and cheer
of the major key. The nuns sing the Magnificat antiphon in four-part harmony at
Vespers, and the polyphonic sound has an extraordinary impact against the unitary
plainchant that prevails for 363 days a year (Easter is also marked by polyphony).
Yet, for all the features of celebration, the day retains its spaciousness and simplicity.
There is still ample time for solitude; the gift is given and received in silence.

I recognise that this kind of experience of a deeply contemplative Christmas is
not open to all: many are precluded by family or parish commitments from with-

drawing into religious community at this time of year (and others would not want to do so). And, in the West at least, where religious communities are experiencing decline (mirroring that of the wider Church) it is unclear how much longer they will be able to sustain this kind of hospitality – although the hunger for it shows no sign of abating, and perhaps is even growing, as the pace of secular life increases and the spaces for retreat and contemplation are eroded. Whether or not religious communities survive in their existing forms (which seems increasingly unlikely), they offer both a witness and a challenge to seek ways of communal living marked by respect for the solitude of each person, hospitality to the stranger, the cultivation of silence and simplicity and the rhythmic balance and right ordering of time and material goods. These are lessons for every day of the year, but they surely have particular resonance and significance at Christmas.

Nicola Slee

Chapter Three
Solitary Christmases

Not everyone spends Christmas with others. Many people spend at least the day itself, and perhaps the whole festival, alone – either through choice or through happenstance. Some people find this painful and want to be with others. Others actively and positively *choose* to be alone – even though this flies in the face of social and family pressures to be convivial and sociable at Christmas time. The pieces in this chapter are all written by those who have experienced Christmas, often many Christmases, alone. They explore the challenges of a solitary Christmas, its vulnerability and pain, but they also celebrate the richness, joys and rewards of facing one's aloneness at this time of the year.

Negotiating the bleak midwinter

Somewhere around the beginning of December, a hole appears in my life. It is the kind of hole that requires sturdy bollards and much red and white tape around its perimeter to prevent accidental fatality.

So I make a small altar and light a daily candle. I find myself remembering the anticipation, restlessness and sheer physical discomfort of the last month of pregnancy. I remember long, complicated, boring journeys, undertaken with the expectation of wondrous happenings – the first glimpse of the sea, connection with a friend not seen for too long. I remember long nights of waiting, not expecting anything to happen at all.

On 24th December, at 7 pm, I walk alone through a hectic city centre that glows green, red, gold, silver. Bars vomit heavy bass beats and tipsy Santas on to shining pavements, and antlered twenty-somethings clutch each other shrieking. A group of navel-ringed fairies sing seasonal songs as they weave through hooting, polluting, rumbling, grumbling, nowhere-to-park traffic. The church bells can't be heard until the church is just a few yards away. Once, their wild changes would have drawn people for miles. Worshippers would have trudged through snow, across bitter moors. Arriving, they would leave outside in the thick dark the knowledge that the food, fuel, children might not last until spring, and enter a painted nave ablaze with warmth and light. Modern cold and dark, just as difficult to dispel, is also better left in the porch. Outside, the brash city can be seen from space. It writes on the night sky: *We don't need you, Son, we can do it for ourselves, anytime.* Inside, we are not so sure: candlelight admits to shadows and we are here to hear the message of the angels. We sing mightily for the sun's return, and with hope that this time He will bring (please) peace, comfort and goodwill.

Home again, I decorate my altar with holly and ivy. I open thoughtful gifts from friends who know me well. Oh joy! Lavender bags shaped like stars and moons. For on 25th December I clean my house. I dance with the morning, sing through the afternoon – all my favourite tunes (only a little bit louder than usual). I open windows and let cold draughts scour away the detritus of last year; end the day with a satisfying car boot full of stuff for recycling, and the clean scent of lavender when the air in my living space moves. Then, a feast of favourite, cholesterol-rich comfort food, a trashy indulgent novel and early bed.

26th December sees the return of friends, the return of shared conviviality. I continue to light my candles. The three kings are still travelling, and there will still be need to break ice on the bird bath and give hot soup to the hungry. But, on the whole, all things considered, it seems fair to say that another bleak midwinter has been successfully negotiated.

Floe Shakespeare

A widow's Christmas

Christmas? Christmas? Oh, you mean the time of year when I spend more than I earn, eat more than my size 16 hips can afford and drink more than my liver (presumably also a size 16) can tolerate? The time of year when idealised family images are ubiquitous, exacerbating my situation as a childless, middle-aged widow? The time of year when I'm always run particularly ragged combining work with my part-time university studies? (And what sadist decreed that essays should be written over the Christmas period? Presumably not Father Christmas.)

Okay, I'll admit that I've written the foregoing paragraph with my tongue stuck firmly in my cheek, but it nonetheless does express the confusion and heightened emotions that I feel as Santa starts grooming Rudolph for the annual marathon. Christmas became stressful for me following the death of my husband, Philip, from cancer in 1996. Prior to that, we had enjoyed sharing the preparation for what was always a festive and joyful period. We regularly entertained our parents and my sister and her family, making it a busy time of shopping, cooking and general merriment. My nephew and niece, as children, were always an integral part of the proceedings, with Phil revelling in the opportunity to play endless games of Monopoly and cards – only interrupted by his forays into Lego and Meccano. He played piano, too, so the house would echo for hours with the sound of his beloved jazz. All that is gone now. Phil and our parents have died, and 'the children' are grown up and living and working in London.

Although the adjustment that I've had to make is one that is required throughout the year, Christmas seems to concentrate and heighten the pain of grief and loss; this is always exacerbated by the fact that Christmas is followed by New Year, the period at which I am always at my lowest ebb. As I'm no longer a wife or daughter, I fret about just what my role in life is. I become nervous of a future without a husband or children. I'm also confused by my attitude to religion, which is also highlighted at this time of the year. I was brought up a member of the Church of England. I attended a church school. However, since then I have journeyed towards atheism, so no longer have a belief in an afterlife to support me. Being a contradictory soul, though, I still love churches as buildings and adore the music one hears in them. (A thought just struck me – why do I still use the word 'soul'? I told you I was confused.)

I am particularly blessed in that I have many loving friends and a supportive family, and so I need never be alone any weekend of the year, let alone Christmas, if I don't wish it. However, still being contradictory, I have discovered that I often feel most alone when I am part of a group. The very loneliness that these kind people wish to dispel is exacerbated for me by feelings of somehow being surplus to requirements.

Oh dear. I'm sorry if this all sounds very downbeat, but I'm just trying to sketch my circumstances, and the ways in which I am now dealing with them. The worst of the pain of Phil's loss has subsided (though I have to tell you that dealing with grief never gets easy; it just becomes 'easier'). I have plenty to keep me busy, and as much socialising as I choose to enjoy. Now, it is at this point that I have a confession to make, one that will probably horrify my nearest and dearest. Last Christmas, I told fibs to a lot of very nice people. I told person 'A' that I was spending Christmas with person 'B' and vice versa, and instead spent it alone at home – apart from the company of my greyhound, that is. Sorry, everyone. And why did I choose to be so underhand and deceitful? I wanted to prove to myself that I could manage alone, and I didn't want people worrying about me. I cooked a lovely meal and drank an excellent bottle of wine; I sorted out a schedule of music, radio and TV, and had several books available too. Of course, I realise how fortunate I am to have the luxury of choice. I don't have to be alone – other people are not so lucky of course, and possibly suffer agonies of loneliness as a result. But for me the day was a completely liberating one. The realisation that I can cope alone has somehow given me the freedom to enjoy the company of others more, because I now know that, although I dearly love my family and friends, I am not wholly dependent upon them. This knowledge has bolstered my sense of independence and self-worth, and has led to me suddenly feeling all grown-up!

As for Christmas this year – well, who knows? I may be by myself; I may invite people round. I shan't spend a fortune, and I will try hard not to become a size 18. I will enjoy being the best sister, aunt and friend that I can be. And, although Phil is no longer here, it is still the home that he shaped that friends will find hospitality within.

Christmas has acted as a marker for me on a personal journey that started in 1996. I'm now looking forward to continuing upon that journey of individual development.

Gillian Ashley

Hark the herald angels sing

My mum doesn't believe in Christmas. Not in the sense that it doesn't exist – the traffic jams in Enfield Town prove that it does – but in the sense that she doesn't believe it is a good thing. My mum has plenty of intelligence and wit, compassion and courage, but she is somewhat lacking in forward planning, tact and optimism, and these are the qualities needed to survive Christmas. Hence all the childhood Christmases spent trying to defrost the turkey in the sink before lunch, her unnerving tendency to tell you exactly why she doesn't like the presents you've bought her and her habit of retiring to her bed with depression. No wonder I don't believe in Christmas either.

One thing she does enjoy, though, is the King's College choir from Cambridge singing carols on Christmas Eve. We listen to them on radio or television, happy together, her singing along in her lovely clear Irish voice and me with my not so lovely out of tune harmony.

They're on soon and I'll be heading home to listen to them. Meanwhile, I'm sitting here on her memorial bench in the park. I've thrown some winter jasmine from my garden in the lake and now I'm just sitting here, remembering – in the cold and damp – and having a chat with the ghost of Christmas past. Not a chat exactly. More of a singsong. I like to think I can hear her voice somewhere starting up the first verse of 'Hark the Herald Angels Sing' and then we'll move on to 'Silent Night' – always a favourite.

We might not believe in Christmas. But we do believe in music. And in love.

Christine Vial

Did you take it with you?

The sleigh bells tinkle merrily,
but sounds of screaming
are what I hear.

The baubles on the Christmas tree
catch the light in pure beauty,
but I see only ugly balls of dirt.

The aroma of mince pies
wafts deliciously through the streets,
but I smell only rot and decay.

The flavour of sweet puddings
sits freely on my tongue,
but I taste only raw meat.

The silky wrapping paper
lies beneath my pale, white fingers,
but I feel only dust.

Christmas has been stolen from me.
Like a child nagging for Santa,
I held my hand out to you.

But you had long since left
this world of bitterness behind,
and me with it.

Christmas will not be the same.
This first year of your terminal absence
will be the harshest.

Do they have Christmas in heaven, Mum?
They don't have it here any more.
Maybe that's because

you were my Christmas.

Melanie Ashford

Something missing

Christmas always hits me like a sledgehammer. I'm reminded that I'm less than ideal and my life is less than ideal, both in my own terms and in terms of the world's expectations or in the light of the Christmas myths. Christmas is the season of longing to be the 'right' sort of person, to belong to the 'right' sort of family and to live the 'right' sort of life. And let's face it, despite disliking or despising the suffocating straitjacket nature of all that, it doesn't stop the annual longing.

Like lots of people, I've never lived in one of those idealised families. I grew up in a single-parent family. It was the only single-parent family I knew when I was young. Things were different back in the 1950s. It wasn't a matter of scandal; my father died when I was three. It was one of those things – nobody's fault.

The run-up to Christmas was OK. I might have been one of those awkward children bored by the traditional parties and pantomimes, but I loved the Christmas music. So did my mother. I remember her playing carols on piano, and us singing together. Then there was *Carols from King's* on Christmas Eve. She would always listen as she made the mince pies or sewed up the stuffed chicken, in preparation for granny's arrival for lunch the following day. I liked decorating our tree and thought the coloured fairy lights were wonderful. I loved seeing the lights in the windows up and down the road. Cards, letters and brown paper parcels arrived up until Christmas morning. I knew I'd get a Christmas stocking. I knew I'd have presents. I knew I'd eat well. No, beforehand was fine. But there was always a point of no return somewhere late on the afternoon of Christmas Eve, as families barricaded themselves in for Christmas, the traffic died away and the streets grew quiet. After that we kept ourselves to ourselves, as did everybody else. Then it wasn't 'right'.

For my mother Christmas was always a time of intense loneliness and longing. Like me she was an only child, adopted by only-children. She and my father's mother never got on so there was no question of *that* granny coming to stay. Anyway, my mother didn't go in for people coming to stay. Relatives who were interested were thousands of miles away. Telephoning was too expensive and email hadn't even been dreamt of. Her adoptive mother would come for Christmas lunch and tea, arriving and departing by stately taxi, and the three of us would have Christmas.

We'd be invited out for tea on Boxing Day to old family friends. Later, I'd hate doing that – feeling like a charity case. We always had to go there. They never came to us. No taking it in turns. There was no sense of reciprocity or mutuality.

As I grew into adolescence, Christmas got worse. My mother remarried and it didn't work out as she'd hoped. Now there were more of us trying to play happy families across the rifts, and granny still came for lunch! But we no longer got invited out for tea on Boxing Day. We weren't 'on our own' any longer and probably didn't merit such treatment.

As I grew into adulthood, Christmas got better. Sometimes I made choices about where and how I might spend it. More control helped. Christmas was the season of 'goodwill to all men', but also a time when doors were shut firmly, enclosing preoccupied families within, and excluding others without. (Only very recently did somebody remind me that the shepherds went visiting on Christmas Day!) I know my mother felt being an 'outsider' keenly – and however hard she tried to do Christmas, she could never dispel that awareness. Recently, while visiting some friends I'd not seen for years, I was truly touched when they talked of how they held open house for their small local church congregation on Christmas morning – and this is a traditional family household, two generations and a third down the road. They were talking of catering for the uniqueness of each member of that congregation and making them welcome. This wasn't some awful jolly gregariousness of 'everybody's happy now', but a genuine hospitality.

It was only relatively recently that I realised that Christmas had always been a time of something missing. I have no memories of my father at Christmas, but my mother did, and missed him keenly. She didn't talk about it much, but I know there was always a sense of loss; I picked that up. My mother died years ago and since then I've not spent Christmas with any of my family. These days, although I'm single and live alone, there's no reason why I should spend Christmas alone; but I remain acutely aware that I have no immediate family. That awareness is part of Christmas for me. Like two sides of a coin, in order to enjoy Christmas – which I do – I need space to remember this and to mourn what is not and never has been. I need to pray for family known and unknown to me. I need to remember my roots, even though they may not be very visible to other people. Maybe that's why so many people visit graves at Christmas, marking them with flowers or with lit candles. What I don't need is to be submerged and subsumed within another family, where there is no room for my roots, however kindly the invitation is meant. Out of my loneliness, I often find myself praying at Christmas for 'those who will die alone this night'.

I still find the 'good news' of Christmas bittersweet. I have no answer to this pain. The family trio, despite the adversities surrounding them, seem to symbolise a shared concern and foundation; one that continues, certainly between Mary and Jesus, throughout the whole of Jesus' life. Indeed, it may have been this foundation that enabled him to go all the way demanded. There's no point in denying it: I'm jealous, as I'm jealous of those who have an inner circle that structures their lives. How can this baby ask me to reach out to all, when sometimes it feels so demanding just to maintain myself?

Nevertheless, I do feel Christmas is a celebration of abundance – God-with-us – or, for non-believers, a time to celebrate the good things in life, friendships, concerns and joy. The pain is the other side of the coin, but there's something missing if the blessing of Christmas isn't recognised. The pain is real enough, but it doesn't help to wallow in it and let it dominate the story. I do not want others to impose their pain on me with no space to hear mine. Nor do I want to rescue others, or for them to rescue me. For me, it is both the sharing of the excitement, the noise and the fizz, as well as the quiet listening and mutual attention between us, in the reality of our fragility, that helps the Spirit be present and that makes Christmas.

Jan Waterson

The cow, goat and old lady

I am single and I live alone. That is not to say that I am lonely, you understand; from an early age I was encouraged to be independent and self-sufficient. The grown-ups in my life would say: 'Learn to stand on your own feet.' What a silly saying. Whose feet did they expect me to stand on? Then both of my parents died when they were in their forties. I hadn't reached the age of ten. It was then that I started to discover and appreciate my feet. The independence and self-sufficiency took such a hold that the person I grew into found it hard to allow others to do anything for her. Over the years, however, I acquired a sense of humour and an endless ability to build bridges and to make friends. Gradually, I was able to encourage people to come across those bridges and to share all aspects of my life.

Christmas has, however, become for me a difficult time: a time when I am quite happy to be on my own but when friends can't bear me to be alone. Consequently, each year I am invited to share someone else's family, which is sometimes a pleasure and at others an ordeal.

These days it seems that Christmas and all it entails engulfs people in a dark and oppressive cloud brought about through overspending, frenzied shopping, the writing of dozens of cards, the wrapping of presents and so on – whilst at the same time everyone tries to continue with all that constitutes a normal routine. But it's a special time. For me it's a time of preparation for welcoming the Christchild afresh into my life, and of attempting to be in harmony and right relationship with others.

One of my friends decided to try to break free from this manic treadmill. She had been presented with wish lists from both of her children. They were longer and even more specific than those ghastly wedding present lists that specify which shop to purchase the goods in and how much to spend. Their lists were made out for her, and for her to give to the extended family. She looked at them and sighed. Not wanting to be a killjoy, she decided to buy her children one present each from their lists, and then to buy, through 'Gift Aid', a cow for one and a goat for the other. She called her mother and suggested that she do something similar: she could 'give' the children trees, seeds or donate money towards a well. The children were to learn that caring for people less fortunate than themselves was important. They were to learn to be less greedy and self-centred: to think about the people around them and to empathise with people in the third world.

The children were told well before Christmas about the cow and the goat; to her surprise, they became very excited. 'Where shall we keep them?!' When the idea was explained more precisely there were tantrums. 'It's not fair! We need those things.' And: 'I told Ben that I'd have two remotes and then we could play together. And I told him about the new DVD player – and what can I say now?'

The final straw came when the 'less fortunate people who didn't have a family' – like 'the old lady living on her own' (that's me) – were invited to share their Christmas. Isn't it strange that I should invite people to share all aspects of my life and then think that it would be so difficult to spend a long weekend with my dear friend and her family? Well, the traffic is beginning to flow easily both ways over that bridge, for the long weekend turned out to be a lot of fun once the cow, goat and old lady were accepted! The children and I drew the animals on large sheets of card and gave them names, pinned tails on them whilst blindfolded and cut the creatures into jigsaw shapes that had to be fitted together, also whilst blindfolded. They never imagined that the old lady could make this task so impossible (she had sneakily taken part of the cow and mixed it with the goat!). Laughter is such a tonic.

Anne Thalmessinger

I have managed it, God

I have managed it, God.
I have successfully refused invitations to Christmas dinner.
I have cheerfully turned down suggestions that I 'come and stay'.
I have said it out loud:
'I like my own company. I prefer to spend Christmas Day on my own.'
I have even avoided rotas and left the choice open as to whether I go to church
    or not.

It was not easy.
There seem to be an awful lot of friends and family
who have decided that being alone on Christmas Day is not good for me!
Many have tried to lure me into the world of crackers, scrabble and happy families,
but I have stood my ground.
I imagine there are some who see my solitary Christmas as a failure on their part
to persuade me otherwise.
That is their problem.
It is not going to be mine.

I've made it, God.
It's Christmas Eve.
There is you
and me
and the cat.
There are books and silences
and CDs and candles.
There is food in the cupboard,
drink in the sideboard,
and a *Radio Times* on top of the television.
The central heating is working.
Upstairs is a warm bed.

I have seized the day, Jesus.
Happy Birthday, God.

Anon

Being alone at Christmas

Why is it so scary? I've clamoured to join in with modes of celebration I've hated or with people I don't particularly like for the sake of not being alone. It's only a day, after all. Maybe it's the big build-up – not just commercial but 'Christian'. It's all family family, cosy cosy, and if you lack a partner, family or home of your own you're a failure. I wish I'd had more courage.

There's a kind of general terror of being alone – or at least of not having the option to go somewhere. A fear of not being asked – even if you don't want to go! Why? Some of us actually enjoy being alone, so why should we, or others, feel guilty?

Rowena Edlin-White

Chapter Four

Lesbian, Gay, Bisexual and Transgendered Christmases

If the fantasy of happy family Christmases excludes singles, those who are divorced, separated, widowed and those who find family life problematic in any number of ways, it certainly excludes lesbian, gay, bisexual and transgendered (LGBT) folk (even if they may also aspire to settled domestic bliss). The norm of family life presented to us by sections of the media and Church is a heterosexual one – although, with the increasing acceptance of LGBTs in wider society, as reflected in civil partnerships and in a far more benign media presence, at least in some quarters, this is changing. Nevertheless, certainly in terms of church life, LGBTs still have to fight against unthinking – and sometimes conscious – prejudice, marginalisation and homophobia. Although this operates all year round, there are particular pressures and expectations in church, family and social life at Christmas that serve to exacerbate the exclusion that LGBTs experience habitually.

In this chapter, then, we hear lesbian, gay, bisexual and transgendered Christians speak about their varied experiences of Christmas – and it is indicative of just how unsafe it can still be to tell one's story as LGBT within the Church that not all of the speakers have chosen to be identified. Since Christmas often places family life under intense scrutiny and pressure, and is associated with memories of family life, it often raises in acute form questions about how well – or not – families cope with the different and changing lifestyles, expectations and aspirations of their members, including – though not limited to – those who defy the norm of heterosexual coupledom and family life.

Queer Christmas

When I was about 10, I watched *Scrooge* (the 1951 black and white version with Alastair Sim) and was haunted for years by the images of the ghosts of Christmas past, present and future. In this piece, I reflect on my own Christmas 'ghosts' as a way of grappling with what Christmas has meant to me at different points in my life, and of focusing creatively on what it might offer me in the future. We cannot stop Christmas happening. We get a year's notice, and yet it seems to catch many of us unprepared. For me, the more I can get hold of what I want and need from Christmas, the more I am likely to find it, and the more at peace I will be.

The ghosts of Christmas past – a series of snapshots

25 December, 1965: aged 5, Brisbane, Australia
I live in subtropical Queensland, the daughter of an academic and a teacher. In this conformist, Anglican family, I am the middle child of three. I attend an Anglican girls' convent school. We go to the High Anglican church in the morning, and my mother cooks turkey and all the trimmings in the sweltering humidity! I have complete belief in Father Christmas, liking the jolliness of church and the crib. Everyone's in Christmas-best clothes, and there's sherry for the grown-ups. My parents telephone 'home' to their parents in the UK; there are tears and joy at presents. Mum is exhausted in the heat of the kitchen and is missing home. We watch *Carols from King's* on the TV, and listen to a radio programme that plays dedications for British expats in Australia and around the world. My Aussie mates have headed for the coast and will come back talking of the sea and surfing. But I have no other experience of Christmas than this traditional British version.

25 December, 1975: aged 15, Cardiff
I love singing in the Church in Wales school choir: there is a sense of honour and duty in the numerous carol services and concerts. Bell-ringing in Llandaff Cathedral. The Eucharist is very important to me. My friends and I were confirmed last year and we are rather pious. Christmas is still centred on church and turkey, my mother producing a magnificent turkey dinner with all the trimmings at one o'clock exactly. Visits to neighbours for sherry and general good cheer. Hand bell ringing features quite heavily. So does mistletoe, and adoring the sixth-form boys who sing bass in the choir.

25 December, 1985: aged 25, Cheltenham
Christmas as an independent adult woman. Living with a female friend, rebelling against religion. Christmas is a series of parties, dressing up to go out, acting very confident (*acting*). Exploring (hetero) sexuality, mixing with yuppies, hippies,

dropouts and depressives. Constantly juggling safety with risk. Scared witless at times and privately missing God and religion. Though I'm not uncool enough to tell my friends that!

25 December, 1990: aged 30, Bristol

I'm spending Christmas in a radical Anglican parish church as a single, bisexual, independent, feminist Christian. Feeling rooted in God and feminism. I've been discovering a new 'family' in church and in Christian networks: MOW (the Movement for the Ordination of Women), WIT (Women In Theology) and CHLOE (Creative Happenings, Liturgies and Other Experiences). Highly creative time with intelligent, committed, radical feminists. Christmas still lonely though, as most of my older feminist friends return to their families and I wait miserably for the Boxing Day gathering of like-minded women and men at a party. Reading everything I can get my hands on about feminism and Christianity. This has been a vibrant 'conversion'. I believe at this point that I have found the community I was so desperately seeking.

25 December, 1995: aged 35, Bristol

I have met and committed to my partner. She has joined me in the Anglican community, which we believe to be inclusive and radical and bringing about the Kingdom on earth. And yet, Christmas still feels rather miserable for us as a couple, as we observe 'our' community retreating into traditional hetero family units. I believe – naively, as it turns out – that, now that women are ordained, Christian feminism will vanquish homophobia in the church, and that openly lesbian and gay people will be ordained, and that the churches will be places of respite and nurture in a hostile world.

The ghost of Christmas present: Christmas coping strategies for being queer in a straight church community and in the wider world

Well, in the last ten years we have witnessed women who fought for ordination somehow losing, or sublimating, their feminism, and lesbian and gay Anglicans becoming increasingly alienated and marginalised. This has brought great sadness and grief to us as a lesbian couple, as well as to many of our friends.

Partly as a result of this, we have 'done Christmas' in many different ways. We have stayed at home and tried to join in with the local church. We have run away to small rural retreat houses. We have joined with friends in solidarity. We have helped out in an Anglican community, sharing Christmas lunch with many people marginalised for different reasons. In helping out in the kitchens with the sisters, we ourselves have felt less alienated and marginalised, though we acknowledge there can be a fine line here between helping and patronising. The only thing that my partner and I have not tried is flying off to some remote part of the world where there is no Christian influence or secular, capitalist, acquisitive hype. I suspect that wouldn't work for us.

On reflection, we note that Christmas usually brings up some difficult and painful feelings. So looking at the ghost of Christmas future will give us an opportunity to identify what is missing, and a chance to see how some of this may be resolved. Rather than waiting – and finding in October that Christmas is charging over the hill like a herd of elephants – we can plan now, in early spring, what we may want to do.

The ghost of Christmas future – a vision of planning and hope

So what do I need? I need community, made up in part of fellow queers, fellow believers. Friends in solidarity. A sense of belonging. I want to rest, and to celebrate. I want to mark the season with holiness and dignity. To respect all the ghosts of my Christmases past. To honour the dead – my grandparents, my friends. To grieve for not having been married, not having had children, not being in the bosom of my family of origin or family of choice.

I need to decide with my partner what is best for us each year. To go and stay with loving and welcoming friends, to be at home, to arrange a group Christmas in a cottage somewhere, to attend an organised retreat? It is not helpful to 'wait and see' any longer. Christmas for me needs to be marked in a meaningful way, and I need not despair at the commercialisation of it but reclaim it, transform it and make it a time of prayer and reflection on my relationship with God, my loved ones and the world.

Gaynor Harper

Silence in the suburbs

I have come to Christmas Eve Communion
in an unfamiliar, suburban church.
Midnight strikes.
The minister invites us to share the peace
and offer Christmas greetings
to our neighbours in the pew.
Handshakes are exchanged.
In response to polite enquiries I say,
'I'm visiting my son who is ill.'
No one encourages me to say more.
They do not even ask my name.
I sink into silence, relieved that he is not here.
The bread and wine are served.
I wonder if they will suffice
to feed my hunger for comfort and support,
to slake my spiritual thirst.
Am I the only needy stranger in their midst tonight?
What other unspoken pain stays unreleased?
I introduce myself to the minister at the door.
I say where I have come from.
I try again to say why I am here.
But his cursory handshake
does not invite deeper conversation
so I leave as I came, hungry and thirsty,
lost and alone,
ashamed of my silence,
ashamed of my church,
struggling to hold on to my faith,
battling to believe
that beyond this empty celebration,
the God whose love became flesh and blood
has heard my silent cries and understood.

Written on December 25, 1998, four months after my younger son
received the diagnosis that he is HIV positive.

Jean Mortimer

A Tonka toy Christmas

I don't usually remember individual Christmases. Like plasticine, all the distinctive colours blend into one muddy brown. And in most respects Christmas Day 1976 was not, by my family's 1970s' experience, a particularly unusual Christmas – we were still very poor: a largish family crammed into a three bedroom semi-detached, huddling around one coal fire for warmth during the day, getting lost in the deep polyester caverns of our sleeping bags at night. And yet this Tonka toy Christmas glows yellow and black, roars like a 50-ton truck; it defines my childhood. Its importance lies in the iconic nature of the indestructible Tonka truck that I was given and adored. Here before my eyes is my very own Tonka: moulded plastic, but hard as nails. Shiny newness revealing the very face of God. Indestructible. I straddle its black driver's cab and trundle off down the hall to the soundtrack of my own satisfyingly throaty chug.

This was, for me, the ultimate boy toy – more macho than Action Man's scar, bolder than Evel Knievel, tougher than the Six Million Dollar Man. The fact that I had one at five has rebounded, like a ball in a pinball machine, through my Christmases and life ever since. For although one might argue that nothing could be more appropriate for a five-year-old working-class boy than a yellow dumper truck, there was one problem: this five-year-old boy wanted, in his very heart, to be a girl. Even as a five-year-old, I was desperate that no one glimpse (through my closed-fingered defences) this truth about me. And so, the ultimate boy toy was the perfect present. That Tonka toy Christmas anticipated and symbolised my life for the next 16 years. For the more I became aware of my gender dysphoria, the more I sought to conceal it – and how better, especially at Christmas, than to behave in ways that signify 'boy' and 'masculinity'? Even now, years on from my gender change, I still work through the implications of the commitments I made at the age of five; and it is Christmas which provides the focus for this.

Being a transgendered child is, by its very nature, uncomfortable; it's especially so in a claustrophobic village where granny is twitching curtains every five minutes to check that you're behaving correctly, in an age when the only press about 'sex changes' is confined to tabloid sensationalism. But discomfort doesn't prevent a small child from living, from trying to make the best of things. I became superb at disguise: pretending to be a perfectly ordinary boy and teenager. Sometimes, and typically at Christmas, the ache of discomfort (the ache of dysphoria is simply that – an ache) coalesced with other factors – choosing presents, family expectations – into a painful knotty blockage. A 'cyst'. The cyst grew fat and bloated, harder to hide. I tried to ignore it. My teenage years were not only marked with the usual malaise of confusion and body discomfort, but attended by horror at what my body was becoming, and an inability to talk about this to anyone.

Christmas 1990 was the logical, painful culmination of the Tonka toy Christmas 15 years before. In 1976, I'd committed myself to being a 'normal little boy'; the Tonka toy

was the sacramental sealing of that commitment. That commitment had just enough energy to last 15 years. In 1990, in a state of depression, as I lay awake in bed in the early hours of Christmas Day, I tried to renew the covenant. This time in the form of a prayer, a prayer to myself, to whatever God I believed in – the God of hopeless causes. I couldn't stand the thought of being true to myself; I was desperate to avoid hurting my parents. I would, then, be heroic: I would embrace this hairy, muscley creature I'd grown into and live as a happy man – at least until such a time as everyone whom I might hurt by changing gender had died off! My twenty-year-old self was superb at making grand gestures; this one had momentum enough to keep me in public denial for another two years. At the end of that time I could no longer avoid the truth. The grand gesture collapsed. My family, friends and I began to talk, *really* talk. I dropped the little boy hands from my eyes and peeked out, allowing myself to be looked upon, really looked upon, for the first time. I began the difficult and remarkable journey of changing gender.

Much of my early life was a process of being silenced – partly through conscious self-silencing, partly through responses to pressure from outside. I could find no language in which to speak through taboos about gender identity. So, I settled into silence. Silence – and breaking out of it – has been a key theme of my life and has birthed one of the theological questions I have for the Christmas nativity narratives: Who, in these narratives, represents the silenced? Part of me is happy simply to ask the question and allow it to resonate. However, another part of me wants to interrogate the Christmas narratives, if not for answers then at least for hints and ideas. If my Christmases (and broader life) have been characterised by silence, how does God speak into that?

When I read the gospels I am immediately struck by the fact that two of them, Mark and John, basically lack Christmas narratives. This is no doubt for all sorts of reasons, but I find this absence *as absence* both striking and strangely encouraging; it is as if Jesus himself has lost his nativity, his origins, his childhood. This has been silenced because it has not been included. Or, to come at it another way: the wholeness of Jesus is not compromised because a childhood or a birth narrative has not been included. Jesus is whole – even as much of his story is silenced. Even in Matthew and Luke, which have Christmas narratives, I'm struck by the swathes of silence. In Luke, once Mary has sung her extraordinary Magnificat she becomes, effectively, a silent figure. Perhaps the writer of Luke felt that the birth itself says enough. But it is as if the birth silences Mary. Equally, the baby Jesus is unconvincingly silent. There is no account of crying; this is an 'Away in a manger' Jesus ('little Lord Jesus, no crying he makes'). Except I do not read this silence as evidence of virtue – it is evidence of Christ's identification with the silenced. This is a God who has not yet discovered his voice. This unpromising, ignominious beginning for God-with-us is taboo-cracking: What kind of God gets born in an outhouse? What kind of God invites the despised (such as shepherds) to his nativity? What kind of God becomes one of the silenced? In the beginning may have been the Word; but the Word in the nativity cannot yet speak itself. I suspect some transgendered people will find their experience of being silenced most resonates with that of the holy innocents; that their silence is not temporary, waiting to be overcome. Their voices have been cut off as permanently as Herod's victims. But that is not my story. My voice may be hidden, but I'm learning to speak. As Christ had to find his voice, so I am on a journey to find mine.

Life is different for me now and, inevitably, so is Christmas. 'Changing gender' was a risky, but ultimately correct, decision. My family has been tremendously supportive and, perhaps, delightfully surprised – they have unexpectedly gained a sister, daughter and aunt. But the cost for us all has been massive, and Christmas remains a kind of gathering up of both the joy and the cost. The joy lies in relation-ships reshaped and relaxed, in the discovery – in the midst of the ordinary annual gathering of family – of the absurd, unexpected grace of God. The cost is wrapped up in a new kind of silence; a new layer is added each year. It is a silence no one in particular has made, but which impacts on all the family, especially my parents. For one of the costs is that my family finds it difficult to speak confidently about my early life as a boy and young man. There is a sense in which my early life has been lost. When I am in a one-to-one with my parents or siblings things are different. I have always tried to encourage my family to feel that they can celebrate (rather than feel shame about) my early life; I try to integrate my whole life into who I am now, recognising that there is much in my pre-gender-change life worth celebrating – but the weight of being together en masse makes the public acknowledgement of my past difficult. And this has something to do with the social nature of Christmas: although being in the present is important, much of Christmas is memory and remembrance. Perhaps, in time, my family and I shall discover, like a delightfully unexpected present, a way through this new silence.

As for the Tonka truck of 1976, well, it is long gone, perhaps suffering the slow, stench-filled decomposition that plastic and metal experience in a landfill site. In my head, it is still with me, though I have become aware of how, in recent Christmases, I have been slowly dismantling this once indestructible toy. Piece by piece, wheel by wheel; sometimes with care, sometimes with abandon. And each loosened bolt and nut loosens false layers of identity, makes space for God to speak.

Anon

Christmas pantomime

One of my earliest memories of Christmas is of helping to decorate the tree. I can recall the magic of the cheap trinkets: the little plastic bell with its clapper; the delicate, coloured baubles; the lights and their elongated, twisted shapes … Each item was carefully unwrapped from the tissue paper that had protected it for the past year. I especially liked the card-and-paper decorations: a Chinese lantern, and a Father Christmas whose fat tummy was formed by lifting a tag that released a mound of red, criss-crossed tissue paper. All of these items were a good few years old when I encountered them but appeared to me very special: precious items to be brought out and displayed for a week or two once a year. Perhaps they resonated with the love of colour and pattern that has remained with me all my life.

The festivity of the season was also represented by pantomime, another significant thread in the tapestry of English Christmas, its tawdry glamour like the Christmas lights and decorations and with the same capacity to thrill and enthrall. And all that cross-dressing! What was that all about? 'Drag capital of the world' is what New York-based drag king Diane Torr once called England; and it often feels like that at Christmas time, with the gender-confusing antics of the pantomime dame and the principal 'boy'. I assume that its origins are pagan, the Roman Saturnalia and all that, but pantomime brilliantly conveys a world turned upside down.

I can recall my first Christmas pantomime, performed by a drama group attached to the local church. I was less than five years old but I remember being fascinated by the ambiguity of the dame, played by a young man. He had made a valiant effort at a female voice, though I realised (perhaps the jokes and banter reinforced this) that he was not a woman but something more intriguing – someone neither male nor female. Ten years later, just after puberty, I was taken to a more professional pantomime by my grandparents, but there the exaggerated femininity of the dame repulsed me. I was much more interested in the group of teenage girls at the other end of the back row where we were sitting. I didn't just want to be *with* them but to *be* one of them. Yet my (male) body contradicted my desire.

When I did finally begin to consider transitioning from male to female I felt instinctively that pantomime, or mime, at any rate, might be helpful. I attended classes in dance and movement, a course in mime and physical theatre, and a workshop called 'Gender in performance', led by the aforementioned Diane Torr. Torr's students are sent out to observe the differences between the body language of men and women in order to prepare them to venture onto the street in the persona of the opposite sex, under her supervision. Her work has helped many women to understand their oppression by them entering, albeit briefly, into a male persona, and has much to offer transsexual people as they prepare to exchange one gender performance for another. In her workshops intense physical workouts, combined with imaginative contemplation, allow participants to get inside the opposite gender by tapping into the androgynous character of the unconscious. The cross-gender characters who emerge for the final performance (which includes the street walk) exhibit many of the stereotypes of pantomime but its magical, transcendent character too …

The concurrence of the Christmas and pantomime season invites us to note the similarities (and the differences) between the two. Most pantomime plots are about reversals of fortune: the poor boy or girl, ill-treated and put down, who overcomes their disadvantages, usually with some supernatural help, and finds happiness and wealth in the end. That doesn't sound particularly Christian – more like the gospel of success – but vulnerability, cruelty and the promise that good will finally triumph are indeed features of the nativity.

Pantomime has probably always been accompanied by speech and music but nowadays the singing, dancing and dialogue have taken over, and the gender blending tends to be elaborate frocks and wigs rather than subtleties of movement – even the thigh slapping of the principal boy is disappearing. But the original concept remains in the word itself – literally 'imitator of all' – which emphasises that goodness, love and fidelity, like gender, have to be embodied and expressed in actions. In a very wordy church culture this aspect of pantomime reminds us that Christmas is a celebration of the Word embodied in a human being – Jesus Christ, God's true expression in the flesh.

Christina Beardsley

Queer carols at the 'Gale

Christmas 2004

Being a church planter isn't all it's cracked up to be. As a newly ordained minister in the Metropolitan Community Church, I was on fire to start a new and different 'emerging church' in Birmingham. Armed with a stupendously generous grant of £3000 and a belief in my calling, I dragged my partner, Will, and our dogs, Bea and Honey, 110 miles north of London to start a new life. We said 'goodbye, come visit' to all our friends and family and left.

One of the people I had managed to convince to join me at the new church was Ben. Ben and I were walking down a street in Birmingham's not particularly attractive Gay Village one warm June evening. I was trying to share with him the grand vision in my head – the spires I was dreaming of in contrast to the grotty warehouse room we had rented. We were walking past the largest of the gay clubs, the Nightingale (the 'Gale), when I started my spiel: partly an apologia for our not very glamorous 20′ x 10′ warehouse room and partly to encourage myself. 'You know, Jesus wouldn't be holed up in a church somewhere anyway. He'd be out in the community doing stuff and meeting people where they are ...' At this moment my brain disengaged but my mouth continued. 'He'd do something very big ... like a carol concert in there for Christmas ... in there,' gesturing grandly at the 'Gale.

At this stage Ben went a rather odd shade of pink, which I decided to interpret as excitement – and a great idea was born. By the time we reached the end of the block I had managed to convince Ben that he should contact the 'Gale to see what they thought about the idea. To my complete shock they agreed.

Our greatest obstacle was simply booking acts. The Christian Church hasn't exactly been a great friend to the LGBT community, and many greeted the idea with suspicion. My tiny fledgling church had yet to make a dent in the suspicion and hostility that is a natural consequence of 2000 years of oppression and denial. Even so, for that first carol concert we managed over 100 punters and even booked an escapologist (we did a double act – 'Vicars in Chains' – which I am still living down!) and managed to get a few carols sung. In all, we were rather pleased: we'd managed to pull a rabbit out of the hat – and a larger rabbit than I had expected at that.

Christmas 2005

Upton from the Nightingale rings: 'So when are we sorting out the date for this year? Is the last Thursday before Christmas a good one?'

I start breaking into a sweat. Could we do better than last year? Or was it a fluke? Would people actually come back for seconds? I had my doubts.

In the meantime, Taylor had joined our church. Having watched, with awe, the military precision she brought to organising her wedding, I knew I had the woman to whip my fuzziness and disorganisation into shape. Within weeks she had come up with a project plan and a schedule – bliss! As we hunted around for acts I realised that we had managed to thaw the ice more than a little since the year before. Rainbow Voices, the Birmingham LGBT community choir, agreed to take part. We found a queer-friendly Elvis impersonator. Two drag queens, Pretty in Pink, consented to appear. A gay African poet, Jide, agreed to read. Suddenly it started to look like a bigger and better bash. Every community e-group agreed to post it, all bars agreed to carry fliers – we even got into the local paper.

I admit to being a man of great and of little faith. I fully sign up to the grand vision of a God who embraces and leads us in love to achieve great things in spite of our own insecurities and fears. It's the small details I worry over … and by 5 pm that Thursday afternoon before Christmas I was convinced that we had a failure on our hands.

But then we arrived at the club. The 'Gale had rented over 100 chairs for us and had decorated the place out. My entire church (of over 30 now) had come early to set up; they had little left to do, so I sent them all out to buy flowers for the drag queens, while I sweated and obsessed, trying to fight the conviction that no one would come.

But come they did. About 7 pm people started arriving … and they continued to arrive until there were over 350 of us crammed into the bar.

And then we started: 'Once in Royal David's City' rang out with Jane as soprano. Then 'In the Bleak Midwinter' and 'We Three Kings', my personal favourite from childhood – although I noticed some of us were singing 'We Three Queens'! Rainbow Voices came on, in wonderful form. Jide, in full African dress, was followed by Elvis, who brought the house down. Pretty in Pink, with hair like candyfloss, towered over me in huge stilettos and ballgowns. Then a collection for the West Midlands Switchboard and the Birmingham Parents' Group – to which Rainbow Voices gave the carol money they had collected in going around the bars.

After that we were all on our feet singing 'Silent Night' and 'Hark the Herald Angels' – loudly, lustily, all together. Then, for me, came *the* moment of the whole experience. We assembled our cast on stage for the last carol. We were all singing 'O Come All Ye Faithful'. I looked around with tears openly streaming down my face. Because there we were, the faithful – lesbian, gay, straight, bi, trans, drag, queer, curious, butch, Christian, atheist, pagan, fence sitter, old, young, middle-aged, parent, child, male and female – all delighting together in the blessing of Christmas. Everywhere I looked I saw people who held a small glowing flame of faith and love that momentarily burst into a blaze, warming all our souls before we went back into a cold world – knowing we need never be cold ever again.

Suddenly all the cares and trials over the past two years were worth it – even if this never happened again. For that moment, I knew that I was simply who and where I needed to be: a simple village vicar doing what a simple village vicar does, being there for the people he is called to love and serve. And in that moment I knew a pure joy and received a small glimpse of what heaven will be like, as we roared together, 'O come let us adore him, O come let us adore him, O come let us adore him, Christ, the Lord!'

Chris Dowd

Chapter Five
Forgotten Christmases

In this chapter we consider stories about the kinds of Christmases that are all too likely to be forgotten where the focus is on material comfort and prosperity, family togetherness, cosy conviviality and domestic cheer. Those who work or stay in hospitals and prisons, refugees in detention centres awaiting hearings, people living in hostels or on the streets have powerful and poignant stories to tell. These stories remind us that a core theological theme in the Christmas narratives and liturgy is, in fact, God's concern and compassion for the stranger and those on the margins. These stories also show that the stranger or the person on the margins is often the revealer of particular truths and insights less available to those whose lives and livelihoods are settled and secure.

Mickey Mouse, Goofy and a fairy
Nursing at Christmas time

I've been nursing for 19 years and have worked most of those Christmases. In many ways, it's just another day: people still get born, die, have strokes or appendicitis, just as they do on any other day of the year. On Christmas Day, however, the nurse's job isn't merely to nurse patients but somehow to entertain them and try to replicate something of a homely or family-type atmosphere. This can be problematic though, because everyone's idea of what Christmas should be is so very different and, for those who hate the whole thing, this atmosphere can be thoroughly annoying.

Generally, we try to discharge as many patients as possible before Christmas Day – or at least get them out for the day or for a few hours. However, this isn't what all patients want. Sometimes those who live alone will start complaining of sundry symptoms in the hope that they can prolong their stay and therefore be amongst others on Christmas Day. In contrast, I have twice experienced the scenario where a confused, elderly person who lives with relatives is due to be discharged on Christmas Eve, but when we've tried to make contact with the family, they've gone away for Christmas, leaving no forwarding address.

I once worked on a ward where it was customary to wear fancy dress on Christmas Day, so we all dressed as Disney characters; I was Pinocchio. It was all good fun until a patient had a cardiac arrest. It then didn't seem so appropriate for the resuscitation team to consist of Mickey Mouse, Goofy and a fairy. The situation appeared all the more inappropriate when the next of kin arrived and had to be told of her husband's passing away by Sister 'Cinderella'.

When I was a student nurse in the 1980s I remember that the Christmas turkey would be carved by the consultant. Those who could would sit together at the table in the centre of the ward and share lunch. This may still happen in some hospitals, but generally the style of modern hospital wards does not enable it. There is no central table and many wards don't even have a day room. There is relatively little interaction between patients as each is confined to their own bed space, eating individually and watching their own private, wall

mounted TV, listening through headphones to the Queen's Speech. Some hospitals still have carol singers going around the wards on Christmas Eve and a midnight mass in the hospital chapel. For those unable to get to the chapel, the hospital chaplain will visit those who request it.

So who gets to work on Christmas Day? Well, generally a form is circulated beforehand and nurses put their requests for shifts in. Some poor soul then has the unenviable task of formulating an off-duty rota from this. It's usually seemed to me that I've been given the opposite of whatever I've requested! Often you don't get to know your shifts more than a few weeks before, so you can't really plan anything outside of work. Imagine the potential this presents for family arguments! And what about the pay for working Christmas Day? Don't we get double pay? You must be joking! However, working Christmas Day can have its payoffs. What better and more valid reason for escaping that dreaded visit to the in-laws can there be than 'Sorry, can't come, I have to work'?

The saddest part of working Christmas time for me is not the inconvenience of working it when others are on holiday, but the number of suicide attempts and the self-harming that occurs over Christmas and New Year. It seems that being alone and ill (or bereaved, or in debt …) is so much more poignant at Christmas than at other times. Maybe this is because we have some distorted idea that everyone else is surrounded by friends, loving family and expensive gifts, which just magnifies the pain of our own unhappiness.

Christine Terry

Carols in custody

I'm a chaplain in a women's prison. We don't close for Christmas, send people home or allow staff time off to see their families. There's no adult education for a few days (this is provided by a local college). Wing cleaners, kitchen workers and chapel orderlies keep busy, but otherwise it's a time when there's even less than usual to keep the mind occupied – a time for many of the women to reflect on the Christmas they *won't* be having, in the face of the adverts and fake jollity on television.

Prisons keep being given less money than they need to look after those sent to them by the courts, and at Christmas the extra money available to make the holiday bearable is little more than a gesture. But the staff on the wings do their best to make things festive and to help the women occupy their time, encouraging them to put up decorations and arranging competitions (anything from karaoke to Christmas cards). This year I found myself particularly aware of the contrasts between life on the outside and life on the inside. Here is one of those contrasts:

I sing in a choir attached to the local cathedral, and in the week before Christmas we do two carol concerts with an orchestra, for paying audiences. The cathedral was packed on both nights, with people applauding our singing and joining in with the likes of 'Once in Royal David's City' and 'Hark the Herald Angels Sing'. It was all quite polished and stylish, hard work for the choir, musically challenging at times – very much a performance and not intended to be otherwise.

Two nights after that, on Christmas Eve, we had our carol service in the prison. Our chapel holds a maximum of 100 and was full, with the Salvation Army band, uniformed officers, staff from Healthcare, prison visitors, some of the chaplaincy team, members of the Board of Visitors, the bishop and about seventy prisoners. Among the readers were two of the women prisoners; and their own music group performed Graham Kendrick's powerful Christmas song 'Thorns in the Straw', in which he wonders if Mary could see anything of the dark future. One of the officers, who was delighted to be there because he always tries to get to church on Christmas Eve, read another of the readings. The musicians and the readers, in particular the prisoners and the officer, were applauded enthusiastically by the women who don't see why being in chapel should stop them showing their appreciation. The carols were all the familiar ones, sung with feeling. The bishop wasn't wearing his robe, and came from the congregation to give the blessing at the end. After the service we all had a mince pie and a chat, before the women went back to their cells and the rest of us went home.

It wasn't a service for the benefit of the 'great and the good', who can take their pick of services on the outside. It was *our* service: the only people directly invited were the band and the readers; everyone else was there because they had invited themselves, and because it was important to them.

Judith Phillips

Lumumba

Christmas lights wink, mock his heartsick gaze, taunting him with merry flashes through rusty prison bars. He sits alone, head in hands: dejected, rejected; only memories to keep him warm.

Filling his mind are recollections of his mother, who prayed a blessing at the garlanded feet of her statue of Jesus. Brother and sisters scrambled over each other in excitement, tore at wrapping paper with delighted screams. But the screaming becomes another sound to his memory's ear: shrieks of anguish as they came, the militia; demanding his father, raping his mother, then shooting her in the head. They got his brother, too – and his sisters could be anywhere. They were pushed into a waiting truck with bags tied over their heads. He escaped death only by chance; hiding in the bathroom where he had just gone to wee. They left; he ran for his life, but was caught halfway up the road by armed forces and thrown into a cell.

Not this cell, the one where he sits and weeps over Christmas – another, dirty,

lined with the blood of other interrogations. They beat him badly that day, with rifle butts and with practised punches. Face swollen, feet badly bruised, he crawled to the guard for a bribe; fled his country with a shattered heart; came here for help.

His case was refused, his appeal was discarded; then followed a pleading to the judge for reasons of humanity, but the judge was having a bad day. The pennies he was paid every month for survival were snatched away by governmental hands. So, left with no choice, he worked illegally – in a factory, doing something that no one else wanted to do.

Then, one day, a swarm of investigators arrived: policemen, immigration officials and suits from Work and Pensions. When they came to Lumumba, he begged them with tears, but they handcuffed him, told him he had failed and now must be deported. The screaming started again; they detained him inside this dark and lonely cubicle.

Now he sits, head in hands, eyes closed, cheeks wet, hearing songs of seasonal spirit taunting him from behind a locked steel door. The guards go home to their turkey dinner and Lumumba sits alone, waiting.

Deborah Headspeath

A Christmas of stark contrasts

It was soon after my husband's death, my eldest son was in Japan, and it was not my turn to have the grandchildren and their parents on Christmas Day. A friend came to my rescue and involved me in an unusual Christmas experience. We participated in a very moving mass in Holloway women's prison where my friend was a part-time chaplain. The music was played on guitars and the inmates had made cards not only for themselves but also for visitors; most remarkable of all were the mothers with babies who, at the kiss of peace, handed round their babies amongst themselves for a kiss.

The mass was celebrated by the liberationist bishop Victor Guazzelli, who preached briefly (in half a dozen languages) and then offered everyone general absolution if they so wished. It seemed ironic that we had to be among the least privileged to gain this privilege, much sought after by both the laity and hierarchy but denied by Rome, except in very rare circumstances.

It was a bittersweet occasion. There was some joy in participating in a feast that symbolises new life and hope but much sadness among these women. So many of them had children from whom they were separated. Particularly heartrending were the black women who, in an attempt to help their families who were in great want, had been caught smuggling drugs and whose relations now refused to have anything to do with them.

After leaving the prison – after a great deal of clanging doors and keys – we had a simple but excellent traditional lunch in a religious community's house in Fulham and then walked round the nearby Chelsea harbour, one of the richest enclaves in London. The contrast between the deprivation of the prisoners and the opulence of this area was very striking and underlined the wisdom of the call for the 'preferential option for the poor'.

Ianthe Pratt

Christmas soup kitchen

Christmas would be different. It had all been discussed and decided. Our kids were getting far too worldly and demanding. It was time they saw how the other half had to live! Their wish lists would be drastically pruned and we would resist their entreaties to buy a colour TV. A brand new short-stay hostel for the homeless had just been opened downtown. We would contact the warden and arrange to pay a visit with some Christmas cheer. We spent all day in the kitchen stirring hearty homemade soup, making granary loaves and baking mountains of mince pies and sausage rolls.

At teatime on Christmas Eve we loaded up the car and took our kids and our cooking to the hostel door. The warden showed me to the kitchen so that I could heat up the soup, while the rest of the family went on a conducted tour. The kitchen table was heaped up with bags of satsumas and boxes of dates. The fridge was full of pots of yoghurt and cartons of cream with sell-by dates that would soon expire – they had just received a delivery from our local Marks & Spencer.

My husband returned with two of the residents, whom he had persuaded to sample our food.

'I'll try some of that soup but I don't want that bread. I can't stand all that whole-food crap. It's full of bits that get under your teeth!'

I served the soup in silence with a slice of white bread from one of the packets piled up under the table.

'I suppose I'd better have another mince pie. And put some cream on it, will you? It'll all go off by tomorrow if we don't get it down us! Take some for your lads, will you, love? They'll like it with a bit of jelly and fruit. You'll be doing us a favour if you take some of it away.'

A box was promptly filled with bags of satsumas and cartons of double cream.

'I'll take my soup with me, if you don't mind. I'm watching the telly with your lads and I said I wouldn't be long.'

When no one else came I turned off the gas and we went to collect our sons. There they were on the floor in the communal lounge, sprawled in front of a colour television set, eating bars of chocolate and watching cartoons! We knew that it would be hopeless to try to get them to leave so we sat down with them, feeling quite embarrassed and ill at ease. Other residents wandered in and the man who had befriended our sons introduced them to his mates. They were all perfectly relaxed on their own territory, away from our 'Christmas soup kitchen' notions of what might be good for them and good for our sons to see.

Two hours later we managed to drag our children home for bed. 'Mummy, you said those people were poor but they've got a colour telly. When can we go to see them again? Jim said we could call in anytime we like.'

We explained that the people who had set up the hostel had tried very hard to make it like a real home, with lots of special treats that you didn't have if you lived rough on the streets. We knew that the subject of buying a colour television for our home would not be allowed to go away.

'It was very kind of them to let us watch it with them and to give us all that fruit and cream to take home. Jim said that he really likes jelly. Can we make some in the rabbit mould and take it with us next time we go?'

It was quite a while before we got our colour television but we often made jelly rabbits and fairy cakes for Jim and his friends, and each time we sat in their lounge to share in these impromptu party meals in front of their telly, we were reminded of what we had learned. Never again did we go a-calling with pans of hearty soup and cobs of granary bread.

Years later, when he left home for the first time, my elder son told us that he would not be coming home for our family celebrations. 'My Christmas will be very different this year,' he announced with a twinkle in his eye. 'I'm having a bedsitters' banquet for lots of my friends who can't or don't want to go home, and you can come too – if you promise not to bring soup and granary bread!' We were a very mixed bunch, but the day went with a swing and we raised a glass or two in honour of all we'd received from Jim.

Jean Mortimer

Chapter Six
Global Christmases

Christmas looks very different in different parts of the globe. Customs associated with Christmas vary, although, as several accounts in this chapter narrate, the export of Western imagery, practices and assumptions has led to some bizarre and singularly inappropriate patterns of Christmas celebration in parts of the world where indigenous customs were for centuries suppressed and are only gradually re-emerging. In countries where Christianity is not the dominant religion, there is little or nothing in public social life to mark out the season and this in itself can come as something of a relief to those accustomed to the media and commercial Christmas takeover in the West. Being away from home at Christmas and participating in different social customs and celebrations can be a powerful and poignant experience, bringing new understanding and awareness of one's own limited horizons. Being with those who have very little of the world's goods yet manage to celebrate with exuberant conviviality and generous hospitality puts a different perspective on the compulsive overspending of rich, Western countries. Paradoxically, being away from home and family can lead to a new appreciation of those aspects of Christmas custom and socialising that one always hated when one was at home! Listening to the experiences of Christians in different parts of the world to whom Christmas may mean something very different can expand our consciousness and awareness even if we haven't travelled away from home ourselves. In this chapter, we listen to a variety of experiences of Christmas around the globe.

African Christmas

When I think of Christmas as celebrated by those who are non-African and non-tropical, I wonder how the birth of Jesus came to be associated with midwinter. The stories in the gospels do not indicate birth in midwinter or mention anything about midwinter rituals. But this is perhaps beside the point. Those of us living along the equator have no experience of the four seasons. It is summer all year round along the equator. So it makes little sense to peg the birth of Christ to cultural rituals associated with winter.

Turning to another point, many cultures do not celebrate birthdays. Rather, initiation into adulthood is much more important. In the liturgical calendar introduced to Africa through the modern missionary enterprise, the celebration of Christ's birthday became normative, whereas Mary and Joseph would not have celebrated the birthdays of Jesus. We read about Herod celebrating a birthday, like the Roman rulers, but nobody else. This seems to have been a pastime of the rich and powerful. How did the norms of the elite become associated with lowly Jesus? Perhaps Christianity was perverted as it shifted from a cult of the minority and the oppressed to the religion of the elite and the aristocracy. Can Christianity regain its apostolic status and public profile? I doubt it, because in many of the industrialised countries Christianity is the established religion of the state. This remains the position in Britain, where the Church of England remains the church of the realm, despite the fact that only a tiny percentage goes to church or takes Anglicanism seriously. What does it mean to live in a country where the official state religion is followed by a tiny minority? What does the pomp and show of Westminster, Lambeth and Canterbury signify in a country where the churches are empty on Sundays?

Jesus was associated with sinners, outcasts and misfits of society. Those are the people to whom he gave hope and courage to continue living despite the odds against them. Today formal Christianity tends to be associated with wealth, power, might and empire. Is this the faith that Jesus brought? Is the Church as we know it today the sort of exemplary society Jesus intended his disciples to lead? If we can answer these questions satisfactorily, perhaps we can get closer to what Christmas ought to be. For Africa, it certainly would have nothing to do with Christmas trees and Boxing Day. It would have nothing to do with birthday celebrations. I even wonder whether there would be any Christmas at all! There might be a public holiday, which all of us who have to work hard would look forward to. But it might not be associated with Jesus of Nazareth.

Until a few years ago, the East African Safari Motor Rally was conducted during the Easter weekend, from Thursday through Good Friday to Easter Monday. Most East Africans looked forward each year to watching the rally drivers as they manoeuvred their vehicles through the mud along very rough roads. Easter is the wettest season in East Africa! The passion of Christ was overshadowed by the gruelling struggle between drivers and their machines. The Finns earned a reputation for winning the trophies. So instead of celebrating Christ, the heroes would be the flying Finns. Before the Finns came onto the scene, the champion was a Sikh. His name was Joginder Singh. So during Easter we would celebrate the achievements of the flying Sikh. This tradition was broken when the Safari Rally was put in the 'liturgical calendar' of international rallying and lost its unique character.

As far as Christmas and Easter are concerned, much as they are part of European cultural and religious heritage, they are a long way from becoming internalised in African Christianity.

Jesse N.K. Mugambi

Christmas in Zimbabwe, 1985

It is five years after independence, five years after Rhodesia became Zimbabwe, but the after effects of having been a British colony are still highly visible – for instance, it is possible, if you find the right shop, to buy Marmite, that quintessential British comestible.

In early December the temperature is in the high nineties, as is the humidity – it's the middle of the rainy season and everyone is delighted because it's the first good rains for several years. And Christmas approaches … After sweating in the heat and humidity, the air-conditioned space of Harare's largest department store is a welcome relief; but there is a jolting mental dislocation when walking into a soundscape which includes Bing Crosby crooning, 'I'm dreaming of a white Christmas, just like the ones I used to know', in a place which has never seen snow – a place where the children complain of the cold when the temperature drops to that of an averagely pleasant, English spring day.

More dislocations are to come. The section selling Christmas cards has quite a selection of visual images: holly in the snow, a robin in the snow (an English robin, that is, not one of the southern African varieties), Salisbury Cathedral in the snow (that's Salisbury, England, not Harare aka Salisbury). In the clothing section there are swimsuits and sundresses for those taking a holiday locally, alongside fur coats for those 'going home' for Christmas.

'Home' was an interesting construction. None of the white people I met would have contemplated moving to Britain. Those who deplored the fall of the Smith regime were equally scathing about the way Britain had 'gone to the dogs' – if they were going anywhere it was to South Africa, at that time still under the apartheid regime. Those who had supported the liberation struggle weren't planning to go anywhere. But 'home' in retail marketing-speak was collectively, nostalgically, Britain at Christmas, with snow, robins, Gothic cathedrals and Bing Crosby.

This experience set me thinking about the symbolism of Christmas in the southern hemisphere, in a subtropical climate. Earlier that year, I had experienced a strange discomfort at finding 'Easter' dissociated from 'spring', when I hadn't previously recognised (because it was taken for granted) just how strong the association is. Northern hemisphere Easter brings daffodils, bud burst and spring growth everywhere – all nature's signs of new life, and all incorporated into the religious symbolism that surrounds the biblical story. In Zimbabwe, Easter comes as the harvest is being gathered. I had reflected that there might be some interesting theology about Easter and the imagery and metaphor of harvest; but, in spite of years of missionary and church activity in Zimbabwe (the first missionary activity was in Bulawayo in 1859), I could find no evidence that the northern hemisphere symbolism had been modified in any way.

At Christmas it was not only the shops that were in thrall to images of northern hemisphere winter. The local church liturgies used familiar hymns and carols, and all the symbolism was of a northern hemisphere winter solstice. The images were of the old pre-Christian concerns for light in the midst of darkness, warmth in the midst of cold, feasting in the midst of privation; deeper than that, the longing for the return of the sun, spring and the new growth and fertility that would sustain life for another year.

In Zimbabwe there is no fear that the sun has deserted the people. The region enjoys year-round sunshine and it is hard to see what sense the people make of our northern concern for a festival of light and warmth. In Zimbabwe the question is not 'Will the sun shine again?' but 'Will it rain this year?'. Christmas should fall right in the middle of the five-month rainy season, following about seven dry months, but in the early 1980s the rains had failed for several years in succession, bringing severe drought and food shortages. When the drought broke in 1985 the rejoicing was loud, extravagant and long (and it permanently changed my attitude to rain, even back in Britain). So Christmas 1985 was a time when we could have celebrated the water, rather than the light, of life. The coming of water into a dry land, the watering of parched soil and thirsty crops, slaking the long thirst of the people – all these could be suitable images to use when creating liturgies or theologies of the nativity.

I returned to live in Britain, and experienced all the

predictable effects of reverse culture shock, most of which eventually wore off. But some things have remained, particularly an inability to inhabit totally some of the elements of northern/Western culture – and I don't mean here merely an intellectual relativism. I'm talking about an experiential reality: that a part of me has somewhere else – some specific place else – to stand and view the world. And so now I find myself bodily alive to the 'pagan' elements of Christmas, to the rightness of light, warmth and feasting in midwinter, enjoying bringing evergreens indoors, lighting candles, cooking warm, sweet, spicy food. I'm content to celebrate Yule/solstice – connected neither to Christian doctrine nor to seasonal consumerism.

Ironic, really: as our winters become warmer and wetter we might need some new symbols.

Pam Lunn

Advent Sunday in Tanzania: an email

IT RAINED YESTERDAY! Ha, ha, ha I bet you all got really excited to hear from me and all I've told you is that it flippin' rained in Dodoma. Rain, sodding rain, who wants rain? We're sick of rain, it's just wet and cold. But actually it is so exciting: everyone's been praying for the rains to come, and people were getting worried. Last year the rains failed and thousands starved to death; people are still starving and rain is the only way out. It's a symbol of life and hope and the people here are overjoyed to have it. Now people are willing it to keep raining.

It really is crazy here; the first drops fell yesterday evening whilst we were playing volleyball (with a ridiculously flat ball, which didn't really affect my playing as I'm crap with or without a flat ball!). The wind got up; I saw clouds in the sky for the first time since I've been here and I got goose pimples. Being cold in Dodoma just seemed like an impossible idea. As we were driving home the heavens opened; it was fantastic – people just stood outside getting soaked, kids ran around screaming, I ran around screaming and dancing and screaming and jumping and generally just being a tad mad.

Woke up this morning to more rain, which I went and stood out in again. (Note to myself: must stop doing that due to damp and smelly clothes.) Then my friend Francus and I went for a walk to assess the new Dodoma. The effect that a bit of water has had just overnight has been amazing: the place is turning green, literally before your eyes; grass has appeared outside our compound, the trees have sprouted these fantastic red flowers. (I now understand why they are called fire trees – I just thought it was because they burned well!). There is colour everywhere; it's a bit like at the end of *The Lion King* when Elton John is singing 'The Circle of Life' and little plants keep popping up over the plains of Africa. Everyone is out digging away in their plots of land, trying to get their seeds in, so here's hoping there is more rain to help them grow. Francus and I spent the morning prodding with a stick and fishing out the frogs, scorpions and massive ants from the swimming pool. Oh, and the heat! Yesterday you couldn't walk for more than a minute without sweating and dying of heat exhaustion; and today I've just walked to the internet place and I wore a long sleeved top. Oh, this has been a very long email; who would have thought that rain would send one so crazy? Well, I hope you are all well and enjoying whatever weather you're having. (Sorry, I shouldn't laugh!)

Ta-ta for now,

Jo

PS I'm coming home on the 20th of December – for 4 weeks I think.

Jo Perry, on her gap year in Tanzania

The first Christmas in the South

With acknowledgements to the Psalmist

By the waters of the Indian Ocean we sat down and wept
    when we remembered Christmas in England.
As for our tinsel and glittering baubles, we hung them up
    upon the palm trees and baobabs that are in this land.
For those who led us away captive to a dream of emigrating to a better place
        required of us a Christmas carol;
    and those who had uprooted us in our teenage years demanded mirth,
        saying, 'Sing to us of Good King Wenceslas.'
How can we sing of snow and ice
    when the sun bakes and we boil in midsummer?
If I forget an English Christmas, with crackling logs, hot mince pies and stuffed turkey,
    let my right hand refuse to write another Christmas card.
Let my tongue cleave to the roof of my mouth
    if I do not remember the Queen's Speech,
    if I do not hold on to bleak midwinter
as I roast on the blistery Durban beach.

Susan Brittion

Far from her mother's kitchen

Far from her mother's kitchen,
shipshape-clean with hoovered drawers;
far from aroma of turkey and chipolata;

far from the picture-postcard church,
from carols at cold midnight,
homemade mince pies and spiced wine –

gown-sweltering in African heat, she
delivered, caesarean section,
a new babe.

In theatre's sanctuary,
mother, nurse and midwife
beseeched the One, stable-born,

to defend from HIV's ravage-affliction,
this newborn. Turning aside,
her welled up tears spilt.

Far from tinsel and her mother's kitchen,
moved by strange-keened supplications,
she found no voice for praise.

Beryl Jeanne

Christmas in Sweet Home Gumeracha

Do you want to get away from your family, your friends, the juicy turkey with all the trimmings, the gaudy Christmas tree, the exchanging of pointless gifts, rain-slashed windows, terrible TV and groaning stomachs? If that sounds appealing then jump on a plane, go halfway around the world, spend all your money, pawn all your belongings, find yourself a fruit picking job and spend Christmas slaving in the sun with people you don't know who don't speak English. Here's my guide to how you do it.

Find an exchange rate that encourages you to spend all your money

Anna (my travelling buddy) and I were so overjoyed about the pound tripling the Australian dollar that we indulged dangerously at the beginning of our year off. All our savings disappeared in two months in a cloud of Carlton Cold, vodka and raspberries, designer clothes, box wine and meat pies. We were faced with the prospect of spending Christmas in Adelaide without enough money for a hostel bed. Instead of dwelling on the impending cheese sandwich Christmas dinner, we got on the internet and arranged a month of cherry picking in Gumeracha, a small village just outside the city.

Get on a once-a-day bus so you can't escape

We found ourselves plonked in a village that didn't look dissimilar to the English villages we'd just come from. A pub, a post office, a newsagent, a police station, a vets and a video shop accompanied winding roads, quaint hanging baskets and deserted streets. We sighed with disappointment until a white pick-up rocked up in front of us. A man dressed entirely in denim leapt out, shook our hands, tweaked his ponytail and introduced himself as 'Chip'. Cherry picking was his business but he never liked to talk fruit; he liked us as long as we were cheeky and had body odour, which probably ripened the cherries quicker than the sun.

   We were expected to work from 5 am until 3 pm; he provided our accommodation for free and we would be paid at the end of each week. He would also drive us to the supermarket once a week since the nearest one was ten miles away.

Make sure the accommodation details are suitably vague

The accommodation turned out to be a shack three minutes' walk from the cherry orchard. The oven didn't work, we shared our bathroom with five other backpackers and fifty other local workers during the daytime, there was one bedroom with four sets of bunk beds, no carpet, one electric light (balanced on a chair – its entrails hung from the ceiling), a temperamental TV and a table with a few broken chairs. We couldn't drink the tap water so we collected our own from a tank at the back of the shack through a piece of hose resting in the mud. We looked around, told each other it was only a month and stared at some funny black lines on the wall. I poked one and it moved. Like spots on someone's face, once I'd seen one I couldn't stop seeing the others. We were sharing with a family of strange black worms.

Be prepared to rely on facial expressions and gestures for communication

The other girls were glad to have some new shackmates. Unn was a huge Norwegian girl with beautiful blue eyes who loved to cook and watch TV (even when there was no picture), Francine and Christelle were both from Paris and had been best friends since they were in nappies, Toki was from Japan and said 'Ah reary?' to everything we said and Josephine was from Toulouse and was Chip's favourite. She was slightly older than us and was privileged enough to work in the office not the orchard. There was much speculation surrounding exactly what she did to stay in the office. None of the girls spoke particularly good English and I could only say what was in my pencil case in French. I immediately regretted bunking off the language classes at school.

Remember that pain is gain

The work was exhausting. We picked crate after crate of cherries (*placing* them not *dropping* them in buckets) in complete silence. When we went to bed and closed our eyes we saw herds of buoyant cherries. Being up ladders all day meant we all woke up in the middle of the night with cramps; and no matter how many times I chiselled the black worms off the walls, by the morning they had returned.

We were all dreading Christmas.

Accept any charitable offers of entertainment

On Christmas Eve, Chip took us all for one drink. As we walked in everyone stopped talking and eyeballed us; it was so quiet you could hear a dull fizz as the beer mats sucked up the spills. Toki took one sip of shandy and morphed into a red-faced, bloodshot old soak. Chip took one sip of beer and suffered from innuendo intoxication. He proudly told us who he'd 'plucked cherries' from, which was everyone except his sister. We all got drunk, sang Destiny's Child (the only songs everyone knew the words of), changed the words of 'Sweet Home Alabama' to 'Sweet Home Gumeracha', which we put on the jukebox ten times in a row, before settling down to a raucous game of snap.

Christmas Day was to be our only day off.

Accept other people's gifts and share your own

On Christmas morning, Anna and I ate cheese sandwiches and cracked open some beer. The French girls spread chocolate powder on toast and tucked in, coughing occasionally. Unn fiddled with the TV and told us all to shut up when she could hear something; and Toki turned up with a swag bag full of cherries which no one wanted.

Everyone's family had sent a parcel which included gifts for all the other girls. We all opened each parcel together and shared out chocolates, soaps and sweets. We read out our cards and letters and went for a walk through the orchard.

The heat outside was intense. Lizards scuttled up the shack wall, petals curled backwards to sunbathe and butterflies mistook our T-shirts for a buffet. We turned over some crates and played cards in the shade.

Towards the end of the afternoon, just as we were all starting to feel hungry and homesick, Chip turned up with a plastic Christmas tree and a cooked ham. We took a group photo with the Christmas tree in the centre, dripping with cherries. We couldn't eat the ham as we had nothing to carve it with but it took pride of place in the centre of the table. Chip stayed late into the evening and told us his daughter was with his ex-wife this year. We weren't the only ones who were lonely and away from our loved ones.

Before we went to bed, after Chip left with the ham tucked under his arm, we poured beer into plastic beakers and toasted our future travels. Unn had one last go at the telly and screamed: 'It works!' 'Ah reary?' said Toki. We all rushed over, saw a flash of Santa with a kid on his knee, and cheered as the picture fuzzed into black. Unn declared: 'Films are rubbish unless they're from Norway.' We all agreed, although none of us had ever seen one, and swayed happily into bed. The following day, work carried on as normal. Anna and I worked out our month, took our money and set off towards the Northern Territory. We emailed the other girls for a while until the messages inevitably petered out.

Realise you'll think you hated every minute when probably it was the most memorable Christmas you'll ever have

Now I think about the other girls every year on the 25th of December, wondering what they're doing with their families and lives. The group photo is framed and lives on my desk: it reminds me of a strange and unforgettable Christmas that was better without the usual guff that defines it. It turned out to be one of the best, most genuine, Christmases yet.

Clare Wallace

A German Christmas

I think lots of people feel similarly to me. My positive feelings about Christmas – the excitement of anticipation, the wistfulness and nostalgia, the moments of optimism about peace and goodwill between all peoples (sorry but it's *so* hard to avoid cliché at Christmas) – are countered by pangs of emptiness; by an unease graduating into disgust at the tinselly superficiality, the consumerism and the canned laughter; by waves of disappointment, moments of melancholy, and an occasional nudging elbow of depression.

I have been together with my German girlfriend for a dozen years, and our Christmases in that time have been spent either with her parents in their village on Germany's border with France, or with my parents on an English housing estate, and, twice only, in our own home – once with, and once without, friends staying. We continue to feel that the Christmas holiday is a fitting time to see our families, even though, in earlier years, staying with my girlfriend's fundamentalist Christian parents was frankly difficult. Our German Christmases have involved emotional work and sometimes upsets on the way to attaining our present-day détente: my girlfriend's parents will never be able to accept the 'sin' but they love the 'sinners', while we will never agree with the rule book that they live by; but we all tolerate each other's lifestyle choices for the higher cause of maintaining a relationship.

Perhaps it is ironic that, despite this less than straightforward relationship with my girlfriend's family (which is in contrast to our comfortable relationship with my own unruffled, accepting, practising Methodist parents), we prefer our German Christmases. And perhaps it is doubly ironic that it is the pious fundamentalism of the household which makes those Christmases so special.

It is a very quiet, contemplative festival. It unfolds according to a structured and ordered pattern. There are no office parties or drunkenness in the run-up. No one is, by Christmas Eve, the worse for wear. The telly isn't on. There are no flashing lights anywhere in sight. Christmas Eve is a day of cleaning and tidying as though in preparation for an old-fashioned Sabbath. The house will already have been decorated with greenery, candles and ornaments throughout Advent. Christmas Eve, though, is the day when Papa ritually puts up and decorates the tree in the sitting room, which then remains out of bounds for the rest of the afternoon. The glittering tree is tantalisingly visible through the frosted glass of the door, or from the garden. During this 'out of bounds' time, the *Christkind* will steal in and place the gifts under the tree …

The bells ring at dusk, and villagers head for the church for the traditional five o'clock Christmas service. The first Christmas greetings to family and friends are made afterwards, as everyone mills around on the church steps. Returning home, Papa enters the sitting room, alone, to light the (real) candles on the tree, then signals for the family to assemble by playing the piano. Christmas songs are sung; a prayer is said. Then the gifts are handed out. After the gift-giving comes a buffet-style meal – one that is easily prepared and cleared away, so that Mama doesn't miss out on the gift-giving due to major food preparations. Eventually, it is time to return to the church for the midnight service, which is a relatively recent innovation in the village.

Christmas Day starts with attendance at a morning service, followed by a midday feast of goose or carp, with wine, presided over by Papa who reads from the Bible to commence the meal (no party hats, no crackers) and ends the meal with a prayer. Afternoon unfolds gently into evening with visits around the village to family and friends.

I find this Christmas very beautiful. It is reflective and peaceful rather than hedonistic and indulgent; measured and calm rather than frenetic and rowdy. I have written a poem which endeavours to capture its magical quality:

December 24th

It is almost five. It is *Heiligabend.*
The forecast shows snow cartwheeling over Saarland.
The sun goes down on your cul-de-sac,
on your parents' small, well-tended garden.

Your yard is swept. Your steps are gritted.
Your mother's broom rests in an apple tree's elbow.
She hurries outdoors at the very last minute
to deadhead a rose.

Your father is on the point of lighting
the candles on a tree dug out of the Saar Basin
which, from the plane, glittered
like a Christmas card.

You have always told me how the waiting
was hard; was the best thing of all: how,
when the bells finally toll across the valley,
the whole village feels holy.

Sue Vickerman

Christmas in Korea

I was never that into Christmas when I was at home. I have a diploma from the School of 'Christmas has really just become another commercial event', and an MA in 'Why Christmas is an excuse to stick members of the family who don't even like each other together and force them to smile and say "thank you" for the tenth pair of socks they've had so far this year'. So, when I made the decision to go to South Korea to teach English, the thought that I would be spending Christmas away from home for the first time didn't really cross my mind.

Even as Christmas drew closer, there were no real pangs of homesickness. I was as jolly as Santa at the thought of a lovely Christmas meal in a hotel with my friends. For the first time since I was born I wouldn't be forced to be polite to aging relatives, be woken up at 7 am by my little sister, or listen to my mum banging pots around in the kitchen extra loudly because she is stuck cooking Christmas dinner whilst everyone else is watching *ET*.

To top it all off, I had the chance to experience Christmas from the point of view of a country which is fifty percent Buddhist. Surely Christmas in Korea couldn't be the same horrible excuse to squander a small fortune that it has become in Britain? I wasn't disappointed. Korean Christmas is a considerably more low-key event. Some people have trees, some don't. Some people buy presents, some don't. Some shops have decorations, some don't. Some shops play Christmas music (two or three weeks before Christmas rather than from the middle of August), some don't.

The fairy on the top of the tree was the complete absence of crazy last minute shopping. No long queues on Christmas Eve, no running the gauntlet of Boxing Day sales. Even for the Christians, Christmas is a more relaxed affair. The day is centred around church. After that they usually go shopping or to eat out with friends.

Thus, Christmas Day passed quite pleasantly. Nevertheless, I couldn't shake off the feeling that 'something wasn't quite right'. A strange pang twisted somewhere in the depths of my stomach. It wasn't until Korea's own biggest national holiday, *Chusock*, that I realised what it was.

Many Koreans, particularly the women, dread *Chusock* the way that we dread Christmas. It's not a holiday for them as they are too busy preparing food and being stuck in horrendous traffic jams. Because there is so much for them to do, relaxing and festivity take second place.

Despite such chaos, on *Chusock* there was a sense of quietness usually impossible to find in Korea. All the shops were closed and people were at home with their families. I watched little children running in and out of the neighbouring apartments eating *dduk* (traditional rice cake) and wearing *hanbok* (the Korean traditional dress). That's when I thought: *It feels like Christmas.*

Like Christmas, *Chusock* has its good and bad sides. But the thing that struck me was that everyone in the country was going through the same thing. Whether the individual Korean loved or hated it, they still took part in it. And it was that which held them together. That was when I truly missed Christmas. I missed being a part of something that everyone else is celebrating too. I suddenly felt left out.

That's why I decided to come home for Christmas this year. Even if I get ten more pairs of socks; even if my mother breaks all the pots in the kitchen; even if I have to queue for two hours in Tescos the night before, just to buy some milk, I think I'm going to enjoy this Christmas. I'll enjoy it because I'll feel part of something. I'll be celebrating Christmas the way I've always done, as part of a cultural heritage that's my own.

Jennifer Waring

The first Eucharist of Christmas,
St John's Cathedral, Hong Kong, 2005

I have been to Hong Kong many times, but this is my first visit at Christmas. I have come at this time for a special reason. In September, my wife returned to her home here for the birth of our son. He was due on Christmas Day, but arrived two and a half weeks early; I first saw him a week ago.

Christianity is a minority faith in Hong Kong, but the Christmas holiday is part of the legacy of British rule. Illuminations are everywhere – many of the skyscrapers are lit up from top to bottom. Christmas here is as commercial as anywhere else – the shops are even open on Christmas Day. But there is a Christian undertone: the tunes of carols are played in department stores, and Santa-hatted choirs sing the words in shopping malls; the media reports the Christmas messages of the Roman Catholic and Anglican bishops, calling for a fairer sharing of this affluent society's resources.

Tonight, Christmas Eve, I have travelled to the city centre – and have made my way through crowds visiting a mock-European 'Santa town' – to the Anglican cathedral: a Victorian Gothic building surrounded and dwarfed by the headquarters of international banks. I have come on my own. My wife, out of respect for her parents, is following the Chinese tradition (which she does not find easy) that a new mother does not leave the home until a month after the birth. But this small cathedral of dark wood, white plaster, bright lights and old-fashioned ceiling fans, whirling on this mild evening, is a familiar, welcoming place. We were married here, and I always return to this church on every visit to Hong Kong.

I arrive half an hour before the service starts but the cathedral is nearly full. As the first Eucharist of Christmas begins, people are standing in the aisles. Those around the door have to be parted to let the procession of crucifer, choir and clergy enter. The service is a traditional Anglo-Catholic one, mainly conducted in English. The liturgy is dignified but lively: the familiar carols are sung with gusto by choir and congregation. So far, quite like home. But the celebrant is the Chinese Dean, and the order of service is in Chinese as well as English. I am surprised at the number of young Chinese people in the congregation, compared with previous visits.

The communities regularly worshipping here, and in whose languages the scriptures are read this evening, speak English, *Putonghua* (the principal spoken Chinese language, not indigenous to Hong Kong) or *Tagalog*, one of the main languages of the Philippines; many women from the Philippines work in Hong Kong as domestic servants. Tonight, this mixture of languages and cultures seems to reflect something of the universality of the Christmas message, telling the world that the desire of nations has been born.

The preacher speaks of journeys: made by the congregation, and at the first Christmas; above all, the journey of God to be born at Bethlehem. I think of the journey of 6,000 miles and the journey of shared lives that have brought me to this place this evening. Journeys, the sermon reminds us, overcome distance. We may want to keep people 'at a distance' but the cry of the Christchild is exactly the opposite: it is an appeal for closeness, for intimacy. Inevitably, I think of my son. That cry, the preacher says, tells us how God wants to be with us, and how God wants us to be with each other.

I do not normally find the middle of the night, even this holy night, a particularly conducive time for worship. But this service has been charged with meaning and emotion for me, more than any Christmas night Communion I can remember. In the day to come, there will be other variations from Christmases past: eating scallops and dim sum rather than turkey, buying cakes for my housebound wife, feeding my son, tensions within the family about what is best for him. But, as the congregation streams out into the still-busy night, what has passed here has already made this Christmas memorably different.

Robert Ritchie

Epiphany in Rajasthan

Christmas for me, for over 15 years, has meant that I prepare for the feast at home alongside preparing to go to the desert state of Rajasthan, in northwest India, as part of a group visiting Wells for India's water projects in this drought-stricken area. This means not only that there is a feeling of pressure surrounding the whole festive season, but that the anticipated culture shock already begins, as the feverish consumerism envelop-ing the feast is a marked contrast with the lifestyle of the people we will be visiting. In the villages we visit, for example, rarely do we see a child playing with a toy.

We do not usually manage to make it for Christmas itself; we start visiting our project villages around New Year. And New Year is very joyful in Rajasthan's beau-tiful cities, with rooftop parties, dancing and fire-works. One year, returning alone through the silent streets of Udaipur, I was very struck by a shrine at a street corner. There were no people there – only a cow gazing in rapt contemplation at the statue of the god. Who says that animals do not praise God?

What has made a deep impression on me over the years is the experience of Epiphany in the desert. One year, exactly on the feast itself, we came across three camels with three riders, journeying through the desert. 'The three wise men!' we cried, asking the camel drivers the nature of their cargo. Well, not gold or frankincense but 'jaggery' or brown sugar: in fact quite a precious cargo in this society. Another year we were staying in the hostel of Project Asha, an educa-tion project for the children of prostitutes. (Their mothers, who felt trapped, begged us to try to give the children a different future.) We had planned a simple service for the Christian feast, when Ramsahai Puro-hit, the General Secretary of the organisation GSMI (a village self-help group), our first partner in Rajasthan, asked if the children could join us. We wondered what they would understand – they spoke no English. We lit candles, sang a simple carol and told the story of the Epiphany, of the three wise men who sought the

baby who would bring peace. Ramsahai then translated the story and asked the children what they thought. It was very moving to hear how they related the coming of the Christchild to the coming of Krishna. 'Like Jesus he was poor, and he came for poor children like us,' they said.

Again, last year provided another Epiphany experience. This time we had spent a wonderful but exhausting day visiting remote hamlets around the village of Pabupura in the Thar Desert, north of Jodhpur. This was with one of the dedicated field centre leaders of another partner, GRAVIS (a Gandhian-inspired NGO working for the poorest villages of the Thar Desert), whose name is Chotaram. We could see how life was slowly returning to these villages, which had not even been on the district government's map. Once regular water provision can be relied on, so much else becomes possible: health care for mother and babies, women's self-help groups (some of which are beginning income generation projects). Women begin to hold their heads up and men do not need to migrate to the cities for work. At the end of the day, Chotaram brought us back to the field centre and he and his team began to sing and to pray: they thanked God that life had come back to Pabupura. Then they asked us to pray and sing with them. Somehow it seemed very natural to tell them the story of the three wise kings who had come from the East with gifts for the newborn baby. As we were speaking, it was not the star of wonder that we saw, but a magnificent orange sun setting over the sand dunes. We said we felt now that we were the travellers seeking wisdom from the East. And what had we found? The wisdom and courage of the desert people which was again flourishing, as the ancient methods of conserving water were being put into practice. And the love and commitment of leaders like Chotaram were making this possible: they were enabling a new birth – of life and hope returning to vulnerable people. As we sang the Epiphany song, asking that the star would lead us to perfect light, it seemed that here we had been given a real Epiphany, a revelation of love and dedication. It meant that, like T.S. Eliot's Magi returning to their kingdoms, we would never be 'at ease in the old dispensation'. But in an extraordinary way, just as in many countries Epiphany is the time for giving gifts, we had received some wonderful gifts. For we had been brought back to the true source of life: the ability of people who have none of the material goods we take for granted, to offer hospitality and to celebrate the most fundamental necessity of life – water.

Mary Grey

Chapter Seven
Non-Christian Christmases

What's it like to experience Christmas when you do not have any kind of Christian faith, when you are a member of another faith community or if you are an atheist or humanist? At least in the West, and perhaps particularly in Britain, Christmas is hard to avoid: the shops and media are full of it, schools prepare for it and celebrate it, children want presents and special decorations because they see their peers getting them. It should not be assumed that everyone wants to join in the Christmas celebrations; some desist from religious convictions, as well as from other considerations such as those we have explored in earlier chapters.

We asked members of other faith traditions – and none – to reflect on their experiences of Christmas and on how they handled it. We tried to make contact with a number of faith communities but, despite our best efforts, we have failed to gain material from a number of the faith traditions. The overwhelming majority of responses have come from Jewish contacts (secular, liberal and reform Jews) – and their accounts are varied and fascinating. But even if this chapter can hardly claim to be widely representative, it does at least begin to engage with the impact of Christmas on people of other faiths (and none) and, to that extent, makes challenging reading. We have called it 'Non-Christian Christmases', not because we seek to define people of other faiths in relation to Christianity, but in order to highlight the irony of those without Christian faith having to deal in some way with this major Christian festival.

Achaan Cha's response to Christmas Day

A Buddhist monk training in the Thai forest tradition once told me of the great teacher Achaan Cha's response to Christmas Day. At the time there were many Western monks in the monastery and he was forever having to restrain their zeal and bring them down to earth. Who knows what self-righteous or ambivalent thoughts were running through their minds as December 25th ran its course that day? When it came time for Achaan Cha to deliver his evening sermon, he spoke of 'our Buddhist Christmas' which all should celebrate together.

Buddhist monks do not eat after midday, so what could Achaan Cha possibly have meant? I think he may have been thinking of the tendency in the East to respect all religions. For Christmas to be truly effective, it must not be an exclusive feast. There must be a readiness to share it with others and, equally important, a readiness to share in the holy days of others. If our feasts divide us so that we forget fellowship with the human brotherhood and sisterhood, then indeed we betray the message of all the religious founders and our celebrations are hollow and worthless.

Yann Lovelock

A Jewish view of Christmas

I feel something of a fraud contributing to this collection. For, being Jewish, Christmas has meant nothing to me; and the fact that it is dressed in a kind of Britishness does not speak to me either. There are Jews who hold parties at this time, it being a holiday, and who might even go as far as buying a Christmas tree as a kind of cultural symbol. From time to time it is the Jewish child in a school who gets a leading role in a nativity play – 'after all, Joseph was a Jew'. But I've done none of these things, and my children went to a Jewish school, so we were spared that particular dilemma. Sadly, my most positive early recollection of Christmas is the sudden appearance of a lot of excellent movies on television. For more than ten years, I have joined a couple of thousand other Jews, and a few Christian and Muslim guests, at a four-day celebration of Jewish learning called Limmud (study), which is certainly seen privately as a 'Jewish escape from Christmas'. From 8 am to midnight people attend lectures, seminars, workshops and concerts on every conceivable aspect of Jewish culture. So to write about Christmas requires me to find a way into a subject that has never really spoken to me.

I visited Germany briefly in November and was astonished to find crowds of Christmas shoppers blocking the pedestrian zone in a little town called Wuppertal. I had not expected the same kind of feeding frenzy there as we have become used to in Britain. Several houses had red-garbed, half life-size Santa Clauses hanging out of windows or climbing onto roofs.

It is true that there was a kind of innocence about Christmas and the giving of gifts, probably even up to a generation ago, but clearly no more. Yet a part of me is aware that this commercialism keeps a number of businesses going, provides jobs and sources of income for an awful lot of people. If we follow the great mediaeval philosopher Moses Maimonides, this might be seen as a reflection of what he considered to be the seventh and highest level of charity: rather than giving charity, helping someone through a loan to become self-supporting so that they can become independent of the need for charity. Clearly there is a dimension of the commercialisation that can be regarded as a cynical exploitation of the season, but Judaism has never been worried about materialism as such, only when it leads to the exploitation of others. Moses Maimonides also pointed out that the things we actually need are few, whereas the things we do not need are infinite so our desire for them is infinite. This suggests that human nature has not changed, though perhaps the possibilities for indulging it have increased enormously.

This leads me to another Christmas irony. As is well-known, the greatest selling song of all time, and the one perennial Christmas song, is 'I'm Dreaming of a White Christmas', which was penned by Irving Berlin, a Jewish immigrant to America. The extraordinary success of the song, with its instant nostalgia, was largely due to its adoption by American soldiers a long way from home during the Second World War and the extraordinary appeal of Bing Crosby. With no overt religious content, it became a kind of secular carol, itself sealing the process of the secularisation of American and Western culture. The commercial significance of the period was recognised by President Roosevelt who, trying to improve economic recovery in 1939, ordered Thanksgiving to be moved from November 30 to November 23 to guarantee a longer Christmas shopping season.

Yet surely this commercialisation has created a reaction, with believing Christians being challenged to seek ways of rediscovering the religious message. My hope is that in doing so they can go deeper than the superficial, and rather short-lived, 'goodwill' that has seemed to be a part of the season in the past. I do not know how the feelings of rebirth and renewal that accompany the Christmas story affect Christians, though I can understand the power of the symbols. I do hope that they point to long-term commitments.

Jonathan Magonet

Another Jewish view of Christmas

What does Christmas mean to me as a Jew? A 'dies non'? A chance to feel that my rhythm is out of step with everyone else's and that this is absolutely fine? A few quiet days to catch up with films on TV and life's odds and ends? A chance for some serious study of Judaism?

Rabbi Lionel Blue says in *A Taste of Heaven* that it's a shame Jews can't keep Christmas because it's 'just the kind of festival they like most with religion, parties and food'. For Jews, Christmas represents the type of dilemma encapsulated by David Lodge in the title of his novel *How Far Can You Go?* To join in the carols or not? To eat mince pies or not? To send cards or not? Where is the fault line between being a friend and going outside of Judaism? To show you what I mean, here are some of the things I've felt at various Christmases over the years.

Christmas during the '60s

We live opposite a family of Austrian Catholics. Each year we help them to decorate biscuits, which they send to family in Austria. We admire their ceiling-high tree and they come over to watch us light Chanukah candles. They have presents on December 6th and so are out of step with everyone else too; but together we enjoy a sense that religious celebrations can and should be shared with those of different faiths.

Christmas 1978

My brother and I visit Israel for the first time. I am introduced to a German Christian friend of his, a student at the Protestant Theology College on Mount Zion. I ask if she feels a long way from German family and friends at Christmas. She smiles and says, 'But this is the land of Christmas,' gesturing towards Bethlehem, and adds that the absence of anything Christmassy in the shops is a real relief, enabling her to concentrate on the real message of Christmas.

Christmas 1981

Studying in Jerusalem, I am delighted to head a page of classroom notes 25/12/81, reducing Christmas to an ordinary working day.

Christmas 1982

On 25th December I hear the radio news: 'Christians all over the world are keeping today as a festival, celebrating the birth of Jesus of Nazareth.' In Jewish Israel, this rates as news as there is no sign of Christmas anywhere.

Christmas 1983

I go for the first time to the Limmud (study) conference in Portsmouth. A group of Jewish educators decided some years before to use the Christmas bank holidays as an opportunity to hold a study event. (This has mushroomed from a few hundred there at Portsmouth in 1983 to over 1500 today. It is an opportunity to hear famous scholars from Israel and America, to meet old friends, to study from dawn to midnight. A wonderful way to use Christmas.)

Christmas 1985

I go to the first part of Limmud, then to the local shopping centre to buy a friend a wedding present. The shopping centre is not a pretty sight – I realise what Limmud protects me from. On Christmas Day I fly to Israel for the wedding. If you can get a lift to the airport it's a good day to fly: the airport is peaceful and almost empty. Interesting to see who flies and who doesn't – El Al and Arab airlines, I understand, but why South Africa's airline?

Christmas 1987

I ask a friend how Christians manage to keep Christmas a religious festival in the midst of the razzmatazz and get a very evasive answer. I become exasperated with an acquaintance who repeatedly asks me if I had a good Christmas. 'I know you don't keep Christmas, but did you have a good Christmas?' Hard to find a polite answer to what feels like her insistence that I must in some way celebrate Christmas – she ought to understand that it really isn't something I need to have enjoyed even if it's a big deal for her and her family.

1989

I'm working for a large synagogue in North West London. I hear from a woman trying to adopt that social workers are very reluctant to place children with Jewish families. One reason given is 'They won't have Christmas'. Given the number of Jewish festivals they will get to celebrate and the ambivalence that almost every nominal Christian I know expresses about Christmas, plus the assimilated Jews who do keep Christmas (the *Jewish Chronicle* always prints a recipe for using up cold turkey), this seems ridiculous. My informant says that no one can challenge this as institutionalised anti-Semitism because before adoption and even afterwards no one dares antagonise 'the system'. I try to check this out with a social worker I know who works in adoption. Another evasive answer.

1990

I preach on the need for Jews to enjoy Chanukah, and to consider things like Limmud, or volunteering on Christmas Day to replace those whose day off it is. (One woman in the congregation took over the local meals on wheels service for years, producing huge numbers of Christmas dinners in her kitchen that were delivered by teams of relatives and friends from the synagogue.) I say to ignore Christmas itself, since the religious message is of no significance to Jews and what they are celebrating is a pagan midwinter festival. Jews keeping pagan rituals infuriated the Maccabees, who instituted Chanukah.

Often one gets no response to a sermon. This time I get two. A woman thanks me profusely, saying that coming from South Africa where Jews ignore Christmas completely she can't believe how her British Jewish friends participate in it. An elderly man says: 'Rather a killjoy, aren't you?'

October 1993

Despite some stressful phone calls during the first days after my son was born, my mother points out that there is, nevertheless, a palpable feeling of serenity in the flat and that it emanates from the baby's basket – is this the emotional equivalent of the light radiating from the manger in pictures of the nativity?

December 1994

I do some teaching in Lancaster and am rather startled to receive a Chanukah card from the lecturer in charge, however nice to receive her good wishes. She lives miles from any centre of Jewish population so must have made a huge effort to get the card. Rosh HaShanah cards to wish people a happy New Year are a Jewish tradition. Chanukah cards were not in existence before some enterprising card manufacturer saw yet another December market to exploit.

1996

My book group meets rather nearer to Christmas than usual. Someone comments on how relaxed I look. I resist the temptation to pretend to be Superwoman and point out that the Passover Seder – guests to invite, the house to clean, shopping to do, (small) presents to organise for the children, the biggest meal of the year to produce for which the menu is set in stone – strains my domestic capacity as much as Christmas tries theirs.

1999

So many kind Christian friends and students send me Rosh HaShanah cards that I feel I must send them Christmas cards in return. Buying them feels very odd.

Christmas 2001

My husband is exasperated by our four-year-old son's excitement at his nursery school's Christmas activities and refusal to listen when told that we keep Chanukah. I say that it will wear off in a year or so.

Christmas 2004

My son takes me into his school hall, points at the tree and says: 'Mum, I know we don't keep Christmas but haven't they made that beautiful?' I reckon he's got the balance right – unlike Tony Blair, who was photographed for the papers watching a chanukiah (Chanukah candlestick) being lit at 10 Downing Street and sends out cards saying 'Season's Greetings'. Nobody suggests that he should hear a Rosh HaShanah ram's horn blown to remind him of his sins so why Chanukah lights? To chase the Jewish vote? To suggest we should all have chanukiah, Christmas tree and Divali lights in our homes? He's known to be a practising Christian so why can't he just wish other Christians a happy Christmas?

I have an interesting chat with a chaplain who phones the Council of Christians and Jews for advice after a call from a student who said that if the college has a Christmas tree, there should be a chanukiah too. We agree that the crib is a Christian symbol, that Christmas trees may originate in pagan winter celebrations, and that Chanukah, a minor Jewish festival (whose original message included hostility to syncretism), is being over-emphasised in Christian countries because it coincides with Christmas.

I write a letter to the *Church Times* supporting the stand of the Salvation Army band who withdrew from their town's ceremonial switching on of seasonal lights when the town council declared them to be for 'winter celebrations', not Christmas. Valuing our multi-faith society shouldn't make Christianity the faith that dare not speak its name; Christianity is far more understandable to the other religious communities in this country than the pagan commercial frenzy called 'winter celebrations'.

We need to get multiculturalism right but I don't believe 'the dignity of difference' means trying to sweep those of all faiths into keeping a de-Christianised Christmas.

Rachel Montagu

A secular quasi-Jewish perspective

I am writing this on the first night of Chanukah, the Jewish festival of lights. Sitting on our front room table is our menorah which will gradually fill up with candles over the next eight days. Earlier my partner and I were discussing having *latkes* (oily fried potato rissoles, traditionally eaten in Jewish households over Chanukah) for tea. The first Christmas cards have arrived and are neatly piled up in a corner. There will be no Christmas decorations. My refusal to 'join in' comes as a surprise to some friends and work colleagues (I don't attend the endless round of work-related Christmas meals) as I am not Jewish. My partner is and, though we are secular, we do celebrate the major festivals of the Jewish year – though Chanukah, for the record, is a minor festival.

It was with great relief that I had an excuse to escape from Christmas. In my childhood though – forty-odd years ago in rural, working-class Scotland – Christmas was seen as being some kind of *English* festival, about as important to us as Easter or Whitsun. A day off, but so what? This may have reflected echoes of other ethnicities in the background (my mother's family is of Traveller descent) or it may simply have been because we were one of the last families to get a television. I like to think it was TV that brought the joys and miseries of Christmas to Scotland. And, after all, we had our own celebration at Hogmanay. In some parts of Scotland this harks back to an earlier time and other gods, with celebrations such as those at Stonehaven where people walk through the streets swinging burning buckets of tar above their heads. My own home town has a raft of traditional songs, sung at the summer Common Riding – the most prominent of which is a paean to Thor and Odin. One morning, at dawn, an elected young man and his consort dance on top of a mysterious, human-made earthen mound. A Christmas gift of an iPod hardly stands in that tradition.

In a way, Chanukah doesn't really compete with Christmas. A small bundle of candles hardly matches the light sculptures that take over the fronts of so many people's houses, there are only about two Chanukah songs that anybody knows and *Chanukah-gelt* (the equivalent of the Christmas present) is a small token given to children. Minimalist then. But infinitely less commercial, less tacky – and there's no need to be brushing pine needles out of the carpet until March. Religious? Not very. Fortunately it is possible to put a cultural or secular spin on most Jewish traditions.

And it is this secular spin that is so attractive. At *Pesach* (Passover), for example, we say 'Let all who are hungry come and eat' as we remember that we too were slaves. I have been at *Pesach* events to remember the Warsaw Ghetto Uprising (which started at *Pesach*) where we subverted the traditional diasporic ending to the *Pesach* ritual – 'next year in Jerusalem' – with our desire that next year there will be peace for the people of Israel and Palestine, and that the land will be divided by and for all the communities who live there.

At this time of year so many religions have a festival of light – Diwali, Chanukah, Christmas. Within the Jewish tradition, light (well, candlelight) is important. The most important day of the week is *Shabbes* (the Sabbath) which starts at dusk on Friday with the lighting of the *Shabbes* candles and ends with the *havdallah* candle, which marks the return from the sacred to the worldly. On the anniversary of the death of a close relative my partner lights a *yortseit* candle, which will burn for 24 hours. We are mindful of another shared experience of candles. The last act of the *autos-de-fé* in Spain, which took place over 200 years, had penitent *conversos* (those Judaisers who accepted the church) walking off carrying lit candles, while unrepentant Jews, or those caught carrying out Jewish practices, were later burnt alive.

I find it next to impossible to explain why I have so freely adopted the Jewish community. Over the past fortnight, I introduced some Yiddish films at the local art-house cinema, was involved in a demonstration Friday night *Shabbes* meal in a former pit village in the north of this county, spoke at and chaired a very large book event connected to London's Jewish East End. Tonight I'm off to my (Jewish) book group. From time to time somebody says something uncomplimentary about the *goyim*, blushes and apologises. Acceptance is one thing, pretending to be Jewish when you are not is another. Still, I've always felt that the best writing and films were from those on the margins. Being a non-Jew happily singing along to *Maotzur* (the main Chanukah song) is pretty marginal. But it feels OK to me.

Ross Bradshaw

A humanist perspective

Childhood Christmases were magical. We would make paper chains from glued strips of coloured paper, and special decorations with twisted silver foil. There would be a Christmas dinner with our grandparents, with everything homemade from ingredients saved up over the last few months.

My parents would arrange a (threadbare) armchair each for my brother and me, set out with a few gifts from friends and relatives. My most vivid memory is of a doll's cradle made by my father from a plaited wooden strawberry punnet, with coat hangers for the rockers and decorated by my mother with yellow organdie, probably left over from lampshades. It was a very special occasion!

My father paid lip service to all this although he was, in fact, a very convinced, intellectual atheist. My mother was a 'comfortable Christian' and a happy home-maker for whom the conventional Christmas was quite a challenge. My father sent both my brother and me to Sunday school until we were 16, on the basis that we would then be well enough informed to make up our own minds about our life philosophies. We did think it out for ourselves: my brother now works for a Baptist church and I am a convinced atheist, a member of the British Humanist Association and work as a humanist officiant and celebrant.

For the uninitiated, the best definition of Humanism that I have recently found is by Polly Toynbee, writing in the *New Humanist* magazine: 'It means recognising that we are all alone here, no-one but us. There is no creator, no grand plan, no hidden purpose, no father and no saviour to rescue us. Anything to be done, any progress to be made, we must do for ourselves. It is all our own responsibility, ours to improve or make worse the human condition. This is all the life there is, the one and only chance for each of us – so we had better get on with it, make the most of it and make things better.'[1]

For years I went along with the conventional Christmas celebrations, but feeling ever more uncomfortable with it all. I tried various ploys to alleviate this discomfort, including putting a top limit of £10 on all family presents and £5 on all others. A group of friends and I would get together for a meal and to exchange presents, usually early in January, and we would call it our 'un-Christmas'; but gradually that got out of hand, became consumed by consumerism, as presents became increas-ingly lavish and ever more money was being spent.

Our last occasion together made me feel so uncomfortable that, three years ago, coming up to my sixtieth year, I decided that drastic action had to be taken. I sent humanist cards (greeting cards produced by the British Humanist Association) to all the people I really wanted to keep in touch with (in November) explaining my approach, with 'Season's Greetings' and newsy items of interest to each family, *not* a round robin! To each of my pupils I sent a note (with their tuition bills), saying that I would not be sending any cards and did not wish to receive any, but that there would be a box for the charity Shelter placed in a prominent position outside my teaching room, ready to receive contributions. The first year there was over £70 for me to send to Shelter, and several notes from parents saying 'at last there's someone willing to make a stand'.

Family members have the option to do nothing at all or to observe a £5 present limit. There is about a 50/50 divide on this one.

On December 25th, now known as 'The Day' (the Christmas period is known as 'The Season'), anyone and everyone is welcome at my house, but my offspring know that there is no obligation put upon them to come if it doesn't suit. There is plentiful food – fruit and vegetables, pasta, rice, good cheese, good wine – and a warm welcome. Anyone who is here may join my partner, dog and me in a long walk up to a favourite country pub, or motor up to meet us and have a few drinks. This takes up quite a large portion of the day, and by the time we get home it's time to light some candles and the fire and get out the glasses.

I don't feel we have missed out on anything, and do feel entirely liberated by being able to chuck all catalogues pertaining to Christmas – almost all of which could be titled 'A thousand things you could live without for the rest of your life' – straight into the recycling bin. I guess it's good to have an excuse to get together with friends and family, but I don't want a substitute Christmas. Rather, I think, I'd like to celebrate it as the end of a year and a looking forward to the next; as a chance to do better, to take greater care of whatever we have – the earth in particular – for the next generation.

Jean Hickson

Nativity: a short story

Naomi detested Christmas. For as long as she could remember, from October to January she braced herself for the annual assault of tinsel, flashing lights, school projects and performances, Christmas stamps, snowy advertisements for mechanical dolls that cry real tears (batteries not included), Christmas cards to be sent and received, trilling carols in all the shops, extended shopping hours, crazed shoppers, traffic jams, obligations, enforced jollity and heavy drinking. Ho, ho, ho! All this to celebrate the birth of the son of someone else's God.

With eight candles and just one song, Hanukkah, the minor Jewish festival at midwinter, struggled to compete. Across the land, every Jewish family (including Naomi's), with very little open discussion of the subject, privately found their own level of accommodation. Some ostentatiously ignored Christmas, eating scrambled egg on toast on December 25. Some joined in guiltily, with low-level family festivi-ties. Others gave presents for all the eight days of Hanukkah and Christmas Day too. Some went the whole hog, with kosher turkey, presents and even a Christmas tree, so that the children wouldn't feel left out. Last year, Naomi had seen ads in the local shops for halal turkey, so she assumed that Muslim families, and those of other non-Christian faiths, must face the same dilemma.

The effect was cumulative. Each year, Naomi found it harder to shrug off the onslaught of compulsory Christmas. Against her will she found herself humming 'We Three Kings', or 'Away in a Manger', though she switched immediately to 'Ma'oz Tsur', the Hanukkah song, as soon as she became conscious of it. As December progressed, and the days grew miserably short, Naomi grew cross and sour and misanthropic, which she hated.

'Could it be SAD – you know, seasonal affective disorder?' ventured her friend Susie.

'So that's what they mean when they put *"Season's greetings"* in their cards,' spat Naomi, planning a winter solstice ritual for December 21 to try to turn the tide.

And then, one spring: 'A Christmas baby! How lovely!' said her GP, midwife, colleagues, neighbours, and all her non-Jewish friends.

'Yes, if it's a boy we're going to call him Jesus,' she took to snorting under her breath after a while.

'A Hanukkah baby! How wonderful!' chorused her parents and in-laws, sister, cousins, the rabbi, the rabbi's wife, and all her Jewish friends. 'Now you'll have something to celebrate!'

Naomi and her husband, Michael, had been trying to conceive for years. After all the tears she had shed, month after month, Naomi wept for joy as she saw the faint blue line emerging and then shining out from the pregnancy test wand. At last! Every particle of her existence sang at the prospect of pregnancy, a baby, a child … except for the Christmas birthday. Should they have waited just one more month?

She vomited throughout the late spring, but sailed through the long, hot summer. By September, she was satisfyingly rounded. In October, when the first carols were playing in the shops, she was putting her feet up in the evenings. By November, when the municipal lights were switched on, she couldn't imagine how she could get any bigger. But she did.

On December 1, her last day at work, Naomi wore Michael's big red jumper with her red maternity trousers, and she found a wide black belt long enough to meet around her belly. 'Ho, ho, ho!' she growled as deeply as she could. 'Look what Santa's bringing this year.' After she left work, Naomi sank onto the sofa and left it only to haul herself upstairs to the bathroom more and more frequently as the baby settled over her bladder. Staying home from the tinsel-larded shops, she sent off for baby clothes by mail order, and watched videos to avoid the Christmas programmes on every TV channel.

One afternoon when Naomi was putting the rubbish out, the little boy next door waved to her. 'I've started opening my Advent calendar,' he called. 'Only twenty-two days to go. I'm counting down.'

'Me too,' snarled Naomi. 'I'm hoping it might come early ...'

'What?' frowned Christopher.

'... Or late,' she said, and slammed the door.

The rabbi's wife came to visit, bringing homemade apple kuchen. 'Oy, yoy, yoy, mazel tov, darling, you're huge!' she cried when Naomi opened the front door. 'It's a good sign. Big belly, healthy baby. Are you eating properly?' she asked, making her way towards the kitchen. 'It's a mitzvah, in your condition. Come on, have some cake. I'll make a pot of tea. Getting excited? I know your mum is.'

'There was something I wanted to ask,' said Naomi when the rabbi's wife paused for breath. 'Are there any blessings for when I go into labour, and when the baby's born?' The rabbi's wife frowned, rubbing her chin.

'I don't remember anything when I had my babies,' she said. 'I'll ask Solly.'

A week later, short of breath and too tired to do anything but lie on the sofa and phone people, Naomi rang the rabbi's house. 'I'm sorry, darling,' said the rabbi's wife. 'I didn't get back to you. I did ask Solly, but he said there's not much specifically. There's the shehechianu, of course, and ...' She tailed off.

'Oh,' said Naomi. 'Well. Thanks for asking him.'

'God bless, darling,' said the rabbi's wife. 'We'll be thinking of you.'

Naomi and Michael waited. Every day Naomi hoped the baby would come early. As the days passed, she switched to hoping it would come late.

'Never mind,' said Michael. 'Does it matter what date it comes?'

'Yes, it bloody does,' shouted Naomi, extreme pregnancy adding to her seasonal bad temper. And then, early in the morning of Christmas Eve, the pains started. She wasn't sure at first, just an odd, recurring sensation that made her want to lie down, even though she was lying down anyway.

'Bang on time,' she muttered between sensations. 'Just my luck. Oh well, surely it'll come before midnight. I'll just have to push hard.'

Later she didn't care what time it was or when the baby was born, as long as it did get born – and soon. She was adrift in the timeless endurance of labour, hanging her head, howling and groaning and pushing when she was told, forever and ever and ever.

And then suddenly there was a bleeping monitor, and a gathering of strange faces looking down at her, all talking in calm, fiercely urgent voices. She was lifted onto a trolley and sped along corridors, people explaining incomprehensibly in her ear and holding a board for her to sign her name. She shivered uncontrollably. Michael ran beside the trolley, holding her hand for as long as he could, calling out to her after the theatre doors swung shut.

When she woke, the baby was lying in the crook of her arm. Michael grinned at her from a chair beside the bed.

'Congratulations!' whispered the midwife. 'It's a beautiful boy. I'm just helping him latch on.' She adjusted the baby's position and moved Naomi's arm to support him. 'Happy Christmas,' she said. 'He was born just after midnight.'

Naomi couldn't speak. She craned her neck to look down at the baby now clamped to her breast, his eyes and fists tight shut as he sucked. Eventually he finished, or fell asleep, or both, and, as he loosed his grip, his head tipped back a little, his face beaming up at her. Then she remembered her conversation with the rabbi's wife, and silently she recited the shehechianu: 'We praise you, Eternal God, Sovereign of the universe, that you have kept us alive, and enabled us to reach this season.'

Even as she struggled through the next painful days of wound-dressing, engorged breasts, rasped nipples and raging hormones, Naomi felt she understood something new. Suddenly the Christmas story, familiar through inescapable repetition over the years, seemed only an appropriate response to the birth of a baby, any baby – her baby. He was a miracle, a wonder, a joy, a mystery, a human. The stars shone over his hospital cot; her family and friends travelled to see him and bring gifts; she was sure that animals would turn their faces to gaze at him.

From then on, Christmas was different for Naomi. She still avoided the garish, gaudy shops and swore at the hideous ads on the TV. She put Danny's birthday cards in front of the Christmas cards from friends, neighbours and colleagues. But she smiled at the municipal decorations and lights put up for his birthday. And every year she imagined pagan, cave-dwelling, nomadic mothers resting after their babies' miraculous births, whose celebrations had borne the Christmas story and other myths we tell today.

Mandy Ross

A Muslim perspective

I will never forget the year I ruined Christmas. I grew up in an average Australian family that celebrated Christmas the way good Australians do: with a decorated pine tree, plenty of presents and a hot English dinner – roast turkey, roast chicken, roast pork, roast every type of meat you could buy – all in the middle of summer. Each Christmas Eve, my parents would tune in to carols on the television, allowing my brother and I to stay up a little later than normal (but not too late or the presents would never be wrapped). Come six o'clock in the morning we would tiptoe down the hall. 'Just a half hour more, then you can get up,' mum and dad would moan, but to no avail. Wrapping paper was already flying around the room, with exclamations of delight accompanying the discovery of each thoughtfully chosen present: bikes, dolls, train sets, clothes, lollies and books.

On Boxing Day my family would pile into the car, holding dishes of warm potato salad and more neatly wrapped presents, and set off to visit our relatives. Mum had come from a large but poor Catholic-Protestant family which had remained close all those years. Aunts, uncles and various cousins all had presents to give and receive, and the same tales of growing up in the Craig family were told and retold, year after year: 'Tell us about when grandfather buried the car in the yard.' 'Remember when mum painted the whole house purple?' 'How *did* dad get the electricity meter to run backwards?'

As I got older, my family changed. My dad moved away and we moved house, but mum kept up the Christmas traditions. It was partly her way of keeping things normal, partly her parental duty. Then, one year I became a Muslim. I had kept my interest in the religion quiet, my new faith feeling vulnerable, like the emerging wings of a butterfly. Eventually, in November, I gathered up the courage to tell mum that I would be wearing a scarf, as I had decided to become a Muslim. I think she thought I would grow out of it.

Typical of many new converts, I wanted to dive headfirst into the exotic world of Islam, with its flowing robes, special language and echoes of the Orient. Once I had decided to go public as a Muslim, I wanted to go all the way. I donned the enveloping *khimar* that covered nearly my entire body except for my face; I answered the phone to my new adopted name of 'Fatima' and a computerised call to prayer awoke my startled family each dawn.

Along came December. The stores counted down shopping days to Christmas, and my mum, who had offered to host the Boxing Day gathering at our house, began buying crackers, mince for pies and various cuts of meat. It was then that I told her I would not be celebrating Christmas.

'You don't have to eat pork,' she said, her lips thinning as she contemplated yet another imposition of the alien religion.

'No, I can't celebrate Christmas at all. No presents, no Christmas tree, no meat of any kind,' I tried to explain with the confidence of one who has found the right path. I had been informed that the only legitimate celebrations a Muslim could mark were the two Eids of the lunar calendar. Christmas was just a pagan celebration that the Europeans observed long before Jesus was born.

'You can't stop me buying you a present.' She was right, I couldn't stop her. But I could thwart her.

'How about, instead of giving presents to each other, you and Ewan buy a present for needy children in place of me, and I'll donate some money to charity.' It seemed like a perfectly reasonable plan.

'Are you planning on allowing alcohol when the Craigs get here?' I asked. My uncles and aunts were fond of the tipple at Christmas time.

'I can't stop them bringing something to drink.'

'Then I'll have to stay upstairs, Mum. It's against my religion to be sitting at the same table as someone drinking alcohol.'

Mum's eyes took on that tired look of someone unwilling and unable to argue. 'Okay then,' she sighed in defeat.

Christmas Eve arrived and there was no tree to decorate. With dad gone and a daughter rebelling, it just did not seem worth the effort. Ewan and mum had dutifully bought presents for needy children and left them under the store tree to be distributed. I had not quite got around to donating my sum to charity, as doing it around Christmas seemed a little too close to celebrating the event. Then, Ewan came downstairs with two wrapped presents: one for mum, one for me. But without the tree, without the sharing of presents between us all, it all seemed rather spoiled – and the looks on everyone's faces showed it.

The next year, I moved away from home. I needed my own space, which came as a relief to my strained family. As time passed, I began to realise that much of my religious extremism was of my own making. I discovered that the world of Muslim opinion and practice is varied and diverse, and I began to learn how to be an Australian Muslim: a Muslim, but within an Aussie culture. I learned that respect for family is an extremely important Islamic value. I had trampled all over my relatives in my religious zeal. Many Muslims celebrate a wide variety of anniversaries, including the births and deaths of prophets and saints: Could the birth of Jesus be included? I wondered.

I ruined Christmas that year, not just through boycotting trees and presents but by being inflexible and unbending – imposing my wishes on my relatives when I should have been thinking how I might love, respect and cherish them. I celebrate Christmas with my family now. I visit and spend time with them, I give them thoughtfully chosen gifts and nibble on the plum pudding mum makes especially without rum. I look forward to seeing happiness in their eyes when I knock on the door and say, 'Assalamu alaykum, peace be upon you.'

Rachel Woodlock

Part Two

Doing it Differently

Chapter Eight

Historical, Liturgical, Theological and Sociological Perspectives

In order to think creatively and constructively about how we might 'do December differently', we need not only to think concretely and practically, but also to inform our thinking with some sound theological, ethical and other kinds of principles. What are the fundamental theological convictions – about God and God's love and the nature of the gift of Christ – which should inform Christian celebrations, feasting and giving and gatherings? What, if anything, might we learn from a study of the historical origins of Christmas? What original cultural, theological and liturgical meanings did Christmas have when it was first introduced as a liturgical season, and how might these meanings inform our own practice today? Or do we need to jettison them completely and start from scratch? What might informed attention to the liturgical calendar and the various liturgical traditions associated with Advent, Christmas and Epiphany tell us? Might there be wisdom in different liturgical traditions which would enable us to stand against the prevailing consumerism, greed, idolisation of domesticity and family? What clues do we find in scripture, in the various Gospel accounts of the origins of the Christ, which might challenge and subvert contemporary notions of the meaning of Christmas and guide our practice? What might we learn from the ways in which different Christian denominations – and others – mark and celebrate Christmas?

This chapter does not attempt to give comprehensive or systematic answers to all of these questions, but it does address them in a series of short essays about the origins of Christmas, the liturgical celebration of Christmas, Gospel perspectives on Christmas and different practices found within one multi-cultural English city regarding the celebration of Christmas.

Some historical perspectives

One of the few things we can say with any certainty about the origins of Christmas is that those who celebrated it evidently always lived in an uneasy relationship with their surrounding non-Christian culture. On the one hand they struggled to define their unique identity in contrast to their culture, yet on the other hand traces of pre-Christian cultural influence show up in Christian thought and worship almost as if they had seeped in unnoticed.

Christmas is not a 'baptised pagan feast', as so many popular books and articles would have it. The reality is far more complex than that. Historians must be careful not to say more than the evidence allows, and the evidence, especially at this remove, is patchy at best.

The first calendar evidence we have for a celebration of the nativity of Christ dates from the year 336, in a Roman almanac complied in 354 using source material that can be reliably dated to 18 years earlier. This is quite late in the ancient Church – three hundred years after Christians first gathered on the 'first day of the week' to break bread and mark Christ's resurrection, and two hundred years after the first indications that Christians marked a yearly Easter feast. Therefore we might conclude that the celebration of Christmas is certainly not essential nor intrinsic to Christian faith. We know nothing about how the early Christians actually celebrated Christmas. The earliest Christmas sermon we have dates from 361 and does not use the familiar Christmas story from Matthew or Luke, but rather the slaughter of the innocents. The persecution of Christians under the emperor Julian impelled this preacher, Optatus of Mileve in North Africa, to encourage his people to persevere in their faith.

In fact it may have taken three hundred years for Christians to notice birthdays at all. Third-century Christian theologian Origen asserted disdainfully that Christians do not celebrate birthdays like Pharaoh or Herod. Christians thought along the lines of Greek dualism that the mere birth of the body was of no importance; it was one's death, or 'birthday into heaven', that counted.

A document on the date of Easter from the same period states flatly that Jesus was born 'on the very day on which the sun was made, March 28th, which was a Wednesday that year'. This makes some sense when we know that March 25 was the spring equinox in the Julian calendar used in ancient Rome, and Christians believed it to be the anniversary of creation. On the fourth day of creation in Genesis 1:14–19 the sun and moon were made. This author made a link between the birth of Christ and the creation of the sun, appealing to the image of the 'sun of justice' (Malachi 3:20, or 4:2 in some translations) and applying it to Christ.

In the Julian calendar, December 25 was the winter solstice. In 274 the emperor Aurelian had decreed the 'Invincible Sun' the highest god in the official Roman pantheon, above the ancient gods of the Republic, and instituted games and festivi-

ties in honour of the sun. So for some sixty years before our first evidence for Christmas, the official state religion celebrated the return of the sun at the solstice. Nowhere however did Christians claim to have taken over a pagan feast: they would have found this reprehensible due to their passionate belief in Jesus, the sole incarnate God – a faith for which many had paid with their lives.

By the fifth century, Church fathers and apologists such as Augustine had the significant feast dates all neatly sorted into a balanced structure in order to prove how perfect were the eternal designs of God. There was a feast to correspond with each of the four climatic turning points of the year: Christ was born at the winter solstice (when the sun is at its lowest point and the days are at their shortest in the northern hemisphere). Christ was conceived nine months earlier at the spring solstice, March 25, which Christians still mark as the Annunciation. By way of balance, the birth of John the Baptist was celebrated on June 24th, at the summer solstice. The weak point in the theory was in placing the conception of John at the Jewish high holydays in September when his father, Zachariah, returned home from acting as high priest in the Temple in Jerusalem. (In fact, Zachariah, according to the Gospel of Luke, was a priest of the order of Abijah: the high priest would have lived in Jerusalem.) Augustine and others found scriptural support for this schema in John 3:30 – the words of John the Baptist: 'He must increase, but I must decrease.' In the northern hemisphere, the hours of daylight begin to increase after the winter solstice, the birth date of Christ, and, correspondingly, daylight begins to decrease after the summer solstice, the birth date of John the Baptist, June 24th. So here was a neat little square structure of feasts linked tightly with nature and the cosmos, already in place in the fifth century.

Yet if Christmas had remained only a feast conceived in the intellect, and forcibly imposed upon local worshipping communities (as indeed it had been in the East), it could hardly have put down deep roots in the felt time-rhythms of European Christians. What happened seems to have been a sort of inculturation, into the Christian faith, of thought patterns, vocabulary, values and cultural structures very different from early Christianity. Christians in fourth-century Rome adopted such pagan liturgical customs as the use of incense and altars, and processions of acolytes with candles preceding the entrance of a presider clad in elaborate vestments who, enthroned, offered thanks and prayers in the businesslike Latin of the Roman Empire not elegant Greek, for example. All that would have been abhorrent to Christians less than a century before. Over a period of time this type of de facto inculturation would seep its way into the theology and policy-making structure of the Church.

No other feast in the Christian calendar has found itself so thoroughly inculturated in contemporary North Atlantic nations, nor with such ambivalent and controversial results. The roots of this inculturation, and of the ambivalence as well, go back to the beginning: the pre-existing winter solstice feast in the Roman state religion, the date of Christmas, its appearance on the calendar right at the period in which Christians were finally able to come above ground and greatly increase their numbers, and Christian preachers' numerous analogies between the sun and Christ (not to speak of their assertion that God had it all planned mathematically from the start). While the parallels do not in themselves prove that Christmas came about as a direct result of the influence of Roman non-Christian culture of the time, they do give us a way to understand our own inculturated Christmas feast not as an aberration, but as a very old phenomenon in new dress.

In the year 400, Bishop Asterius of Amasea preached a marvellous denunciation of hypocritical holiday gift-giving, to wean his Christian community from the excesses of their society. To paraphrase: 'What should we call this feast? It isn't a feast at all! There is no real friendship behind all the presents. Everyone wants to get presents. Those who give them are ill-tempered, and those who receive them pass them on to more prominent people. This so-called festival causes nothing but debts and grief. Children learn to beg and grovel for presents. Those who can, get out of town. Magistrates waste money to acquire personal fame. And as for the soldiers ...' Clearly, some of our own struggles with Christmas have an ancient pedigree! Sometimes I think we have it backwards. The commercialisation of Christmas may serve as a handy blame-object, a scapegoat, but it's not the problem. The problem is that the contemporary Christmas is reflecting us back to ourselves at twice life-size, as it were. Magnified through the hyper-intensity of Christmas shopping, we see more clearly how normative our mercantile culture has become, one in which a high proportion of communications and interactions have the goal of making us buy, or buy into, something. We react profoundly against the depersonalisation, the trivialisation of values, the mass-marketing of our hopes. And rightly so. Perhaps that perception is in itself a profound gift.

Susan Roll

Some liturgical perspectives

Writing in 1992, and imagining the state of British Christianity in 2020, Professor Haddon Willmer wrote: 'I hope that in 2020 Christianity in Britain will have come to make little or nothing of the nativity and Christmas, whose commercialism, nostalgia and sentimentality about God and humanity lead us into annual bouts of misrepresenting Christian faith with the false hope that Christianity can be built on keeping children happy'. [2] Now, in 2006 – halfway into Willmer's timescale – we may wish to do December differently in order to resist the commercialism, nostalgia and sentimentality of contemporary Christmas celebrations, but Willmer's hope that little or nothing will be made of Christmas just 15 years from now seems quite unlikely to be fulfilled. Still, this book may make a modest but important contribution to help to dismantle what's wrong with it and try again! And given that it seems unlikely that Christmas will go away in the near future, this short reflection explores some starting points to reclaiming the more challenging dimensions of the long heritage of the celebration of the nativity in the Christian tradition.

The Christmas cycle embraces three seasons of the Christian year, starting with Advent, beginning five Sundays before Christmas Day. Advent is in a sense about preparation (although not for shopping). One of the ways in which the days of Advent developed was in distinction to a coterminous pagan festival, Saturnalia. As Saturnalia was marked by excess and debauchery, the Church required Christian people to embrace an increased asceticism of devotion and practice throughout these days. The second season in the cycle is the Christmas season itself, which runs from midnight mass to January 6. The start of the third season, Epiphany, is concerned, in a variety of ways, with the 'appearing' of Jesus – particularly the three revelatory events of: the visit of the Magi (their gifts honouring Christ as prophet, priest and king); the opening of his public ministry in baptism, when the Spirit descended, affirming him as God's own beloved one; and the sign at Cana when his glory was shown forth. And here again, a kind of combative approach was present, for, from early days in the West, January 6 was associated with the baptism of Christ, relating Jesus' birth to the symbolism of new birth granted to believers. Further, this date was fixed perhaps in part to contest the pagan commemoration of the birth of Aion, god of time and eternity. So in focusing on this day, the Church may have been making a bold statement about time and eternity being the gift and subject of Jesus Christ.

If you ever attend a 'liturgical' church, look and learn how these seasons are distinguished. If you don't attend a liturgical church, ask what might be gained from giving the celebration of Christmas Day a *context* in the wider setting of waiting and showing forth that the seasons of the cycle together unfold. Then, the question that counts: What might that wider context do to challenge the commercialism, nostalgia and sentimentality of a narrower focus?

If you attend a church that celebrates saints, then there's a further layer of the season that yields its own challenges; for the saints' days immediately following Christmas Day unfold some harsh themes that amplify the difficult things – a difficult journey, 'no room at the inn' – that mark the Gospels' nativity stories. December 26 is St Stephen's Day: according to Acts, he was the first Christian martyr. December 28 is Holy Innocents' – a day of commemoration for the infant children slaughtered by Herod, according to the story in Matthew. In the Middle Ages, the commemorated came to be known as 'the companions of Christ', those killed because of Christ. In the calendar of saints, then, are bleak days that embrace hard, unsentimental themes – an antidote to the monochrome joy of the contemporary Christmas.

Also in the Middle Ages, a further tradition developed in liturgical celebrations of Holy Innocents' Day. As the children of that story were remembered, so in the day's liturgy children were especially honoured by being given leading roles. In fact, the liturgical roles of adults and children – particularly *leaders* and children – were reversed. A child would preside, a child would preach and, although just for a day, the clergy would be relegated to the choir where the children were ordinarily present. What might inspire us about this tradition is emphatically not that the leadership of children was welcomed only once a year, but that the role reversal was itself perhaps a kind of witness to the dynamic of *kenosis* (self-emptying), which we affirm as integral to incarnation: the strong become weak, the weak become strong. At present, in many churches, including children at Christmas seems to stretch to inviting them to a Christingle service, no doubt a good thing in itself; but very often in practice the Christingle service seems in its 'explanation' of the meaning of the images it employs to invite prescribed and predictable interpretations that mute some of the challenging aspects of the nativity narratives: an orange represents the world; four cocktail sticks: the earth's 'four corners'; food impaled on the cocktail sticks: the fruits of the earth; red ribbon: the blood of Christ; a candle: the light of Christ.

More vivid, I think, is the tradition of Las Posadas ('The Inns'), which originated in Latin America and has spread north. In Britain the posada has not yet been popularised,

although there is a growing awareness of the custom. This tradition may better relate the shadows in the nativity narratives and so encourage resistance to the sentimentalising of Christmas, even for children. In the posada, miniature figures of the holy family (which can be bought through the Church Army, amongst other sources, but might also be made or improvised) are 'housed' at the homes of various parishioners through the Advent season, or in people's places of work (shops, offices, schools ...). Eventually they are brought to a gathered church community for a service on Christmas Eve (the time at which Christingle is most popular). The ritual of movement from one home to another of course represents the holy family's journey to Bethlehem according to biblical tradition, and the liturgical text which accompanies the rite of welcome and departure at each home incorporates a strong sense of the desperation of the family in their vulnerable state. Fragments of dialogue include, on the lips of Mary and Joseph: 'We are tired and we are cold. May we please have shelter? ... It is not by our own choice that we travel.' And from the mouths of those who refuse them: 'You look dirty and you smell ... for your kind there is no place, our inn is decent ... For your reasons we care not, every room is taken ... you are bad for business.'³ With the figures housed in people's homes, perhaps amidst children's fashion and action toys – Barbie, Action Man and such like – challenging realities may be vividly explored in this ritual. Las Posadas offers us one of the best clues to ditching the insipid nostalgia and sentimentality of many performances of Christmas and so to doing December differently.

Stephen Burns

Christmas in Gospel perspective

Let's start with a strange vision. Nothing in itself to suggest Christmas, but bear with me. In the old picture of God on a throne in the book of Revelation, chapter 4, very close to God are four living creatures, full of eyes: one like a lion, the second like an ox, the third with a face like a human face, and the fourth like a flying eagle. Because they are close to God and because of the eyes looking everywhere, these creatures came to symbolise the four Gospels: the lion for Mark, the ox for Luke, the human face for Matthew, the eagle for John.

That's the first preliminary. The second is this. Each of the Gospels has a prologue, much like an overture announcing the themes of an opera, or a preface or introduction to the themes of a book. Prologues, overtures and prefaces are usually the last bit of the work to be composed. You have to work out what you want to say, write that, and only then do you know how to introduce it all.

Let's start with Luke. His prologue includes the Christmas story. It's the Christmas of our childhoods, with nativity plays, the child at the centre, special services in church, and family reunions. It's even the Christmas of inviting the stranger, or the lonely, into your house, a gesture, genuine enough, to the ones who feel out in the cold. Now the nativity scene as we have it in Luke's Gospel was embellished during the Middle Ages when St Francis of Assisi introduced the crib and included animals.

We miss the sharpness of the original and all too easily sentimentalise history. Most scholars point out to us that the wonderful story is written not to record the details of an event, but to convince the original hearers of profound truth. And the ox is an animal that is sacrificed, and a good deal of the story in Luke is in the great place of sacrifice, the Temple in Jerusalem. Luke begins his Gospel with Zechariah in the Temple, and ends it with the apostles in the Temple, the place of worship and blessings. But the hint is there that the story of Jesus is going to include something tough for him. He is the one who will teach us to love our neighbours as ourselves, but he carried that out in ways that got him and will get us into trouble: the neighbour is each and all, especially the ones who are excluded. Maybe for some Christmas is genuinely a time of happy families, but it can all too easily become cosy families, cosy at the expense of the one who is not there and not talked about. And there are those who can't cope with more than a few hours and have long since vanished by Boxing Day morning.

Now let's turn to Mark and his lion. His Gospel is all about the use and misuse of power. There is a scary voice in the wilderness at the beginning and sheer fright at the end. God's power has come to cleanse his people and trample on evil. But underneath there is a paradox. The hidden message is that the way to lasting triumph is not by superior force but by being vulnerable and rejected and following the way of a cross. The outcast is around in Luke and the enemy in Mark. But the way of Jesus is to love them both. If you follow Mark, you can ignore Christmas altogether. He doesn't mention Jesus' early life at all. You can go off to the Canaries or the Caribbean for some sun, and genuine enough may be your need for rest. But don't forget the lion's roar – it is like the fiery breath of the dragon, sitting on treasure that it is guarding, hidden from view; and it won't let you near if the centre of your life is self-indulgence.

Matthew has the human face as his symbol. His prologue contains a genealogy of Jesus that includes some very doubtful characters. The message is that God can well use what is worst about you. The family tree goes back to Abraham, in whom all the families of the earth are promised blessing. Then the infant Jesus re-enacts, again as story, the history of his people: a refugee into Egypt, a displaced person in Nazareth. And, usually melded with Luke's shepherds in nativity plays, we have Matthew's sages, sorcerers, wise men, or whoever they were, but foreigners to the Jewish people. The message is that Jesus is of universal significance. There is no 'us and them' any more in his domain. We have to love one another as he has loved us. There are some who do this in dark December by actively helping with charities, such as Crisis at

Christmas, giving warmth, shelter and food to those who are homeless.

John's eagle is the bearer of the Word, flying with strength and power to all corners of the earth, and flying close to the gates of heaven – at least in the old picture of the universe. Heaven and earth have become one in Jesus, divine and human. John's Gospel is a great poem, the result of years of meditation on the significance of Jesus. Maybe it's time for a Christmas retreat this year, time for contemplation with the Carmelites or Cistercians, or, very silent and very solitary, with the Carthusians.

But that is no easy option either. The Word has become flesh. We find God in human bodies, including our own. We may spend a silent Christmas but it can't be an escape from flesh and blood. Love God with the whole of your being – yes, but such love is embedded in other human beings. Two sides of one coin really: you can distinguish between divine and human love but you can't separate them any more. Enemies, outcasts, refugees, exiles, neighbours, one another, including the most tiresome of your relations, as well as those friends that someone once said are God's apology for relations – in and through them all, God. Oh yes, and don't forget yourself: all the separations are overcome. And that's all quite a revelation, quite a gift; and it's worth a toast or two, a chuckle with a baby, a laugh with a child, a touch of compassion that is justice in miniature and brings hope, moments of silence and wonder under the night sky. You can find them all in those prologues: children and church, Canaries and chocolate, charities and Crisis, Carmelites and contemplation – and somehow not scapegoating your poor old family, nor being too self-indulgent, and above all not becoming a grumpy recluse.

Jim Cotter

UK Christmases in sociological perspective

The prominence of Father Christmas, nativity scenes, jingle bells and jollification makes it easy to forget the very different ways in which Christmas is celebrated around the world and the great range of attitudes there are towards celebrating Christmas. A favourite project for children in the UK is finding out about Christmas 'in other lands', now the subject of several websites. Another time-honoured motif in seasonal Yuletide coverage is unpicking the British Christmas, so reminding ourselves of how originally un-British almost every strand is – apart from the holly, ivy and mistletoe – with Christmas trees adopted from Prince Albert's Germany and turkey from the USA.[4]

In what follows, however, I will be taking the rather different tack of sharing some of the rich diversity of not global but local practice and attitudes from within a few square miles of the UK city of Coventry. First there will be a glimpse of the variety of ways in which, ethnically and denominationally, diverse Christian families mark Jesus' birth, and the feelings that they have about its significance. After that, I will report on how young people from Hindu and Sikh families in Coventry observe Christmas. I will mention some dissenting voices in the UK, and the part played by schools in perpetuating Christmas.

At this point it needs to be explained that the field studies of young people on which this essay is based were funded by the Leverhulme Trust and the Economic and Social Research Council between 1986 and 1996. The research consisted of observation, particularly in places of worship and in private homes, and interviews, which were semi-structured, allowing scope for following up interviewees' particular enthusiasms and concerns.[5]

One phase of the investigation involved finding out the ways in which young people from 13 local Coventry churches marked Christmas. These were: Anglican, Baptist, Greek Orthodox, Methodist, two Black-led Pentecostal congregations, Quaker, Roman Catholic, Salvation Army, United Reformed and Ukrainian Catholic. (The Ukrainian Catholic Church is also known as Greek Catholic. Ukrainian Catholics acknowledge the primacy of the Pope while maintaining an Orthodox form, including liturgy and calendar.) All of the young people in my field study identified themselves as Christian and their accounts of Christmas revealed, not surprisingly, a high degree of shared or overlapping experience.

The young people described shopping and putting up decorations at home. Some mentioned nativity scenes at home and in churches. Many took part in Christmas plays at church and in carol singing. Christmas provided the theme for their Sunday school classes and there were parties organised by the teachers of these as well as at school. At home, Father Christmas's visit, family get-togethers and 'a normal turkey dinner' with Christmas pudding were usual; although one eight-year-old girl confided, 'I'm a bit tired of Christmas cake at Christmas.' Children from a range of denominational and cultural backgrounds distinguished the religious meaning of Christmas as 'Jesus's birthday' from its current commercialisation.

At the same time, as well as this largely shared experience, the research also showed a marked diversity in the ways that Christmas was celebrated and in attitudes towards the festival. For example, on 19th December, or on the Saturday nearest to this date, the Ukrainian Catholic children celebrated St Nicholas' Day, and a man dressed to represent St Nicholas (*Svjatyj Mykolaj*) distributed their gifts. If they did not have to be in school on January 7th (the date of Christmas by the older Julian calendar which the UK's Ukrainian Catholics follow) it was on this day that they enjoyed their Christmas dinner (lunch) of twelve meatless dishes (such as borsch), plus cotletta (meatballs). But, to quote one twelve-year-old girl: 'We're allowed to miss [school] when it's a special occasion to do with another religion, but mum hardly ever lets me take Ukrainian Christmas off.'

In a rather different minority, a boy from a Pentecostal Jamaican congregation explained that: 'I don't think that Christmas is true because … God didn't ask people to call it Christmas. It isn't in the Bible … it doesn't say in the Bible he was born on the 25th December.'

His condemnation is continuous with the widespread Protestant view in pre-Victorian Britain that Christmas celebrations were both pagan and Papist. It is also consistent with, for example, the Independent Christian Fellowship, a 'house church' in Manchester, which, to quote Martin Stringer, 'resolutely refused to acknowledge any festivals (including Easter …)'.[6]

At the same time, my Coventry-based research among young Sikhs and Hindus found that they were happily sharing in the secular features of Christmas with committed and nominal Christians and with the religiously unaligned. They sent greeting cards, decorated their homes and exchanged wrapped presents. In the words of one twelve-year-old girl: 'We celebrate lightly, we don't do it religiously as Christ and all that. It's like a gathering and my cousins come down and give each other presents. We have a dinner and watch TV.'

A nine-year-old boy told me: 'Christmas Day we open all our toys and on Boxing Day we can mess about. I like messing about.'

Hearing these accounts brought to mind the study that Marie Gillespie carried out among young Punjabis in Southall. Gillespie had encouraged her students (Sikhs and Hindus) to write Christmas diaries. In these they too reported giving cards and eating and watching television with their families – though in some families the delicacies were vegetarian.

But some Hindu families do more than 'celebrate lightly', and incorporate an unambiguously religious element. While Gillespie reports a Hindu family in Southall 'put[ting] up the lights around a God they believe in', an American scholar of Hinduism, JY Fenton, reports that 'many Hindus in America have told me that they perform *puja* [i.e. Hindu-style worship] for Jesus at Christmas time'. For

Coventrian devotees of Sathya Sai Baba (who is widely regarded as God in human form) Christmas includes singing *bhajans* (devotional songs) in front of a swinging cradle holding an image of the baby Jesus. All these Sai devotees are from Hindu families with roots in the Indian state of Gujarat, and this style of devotion is clearly patterned on Gujarati Hindu celebration of the birthdays of the divine incarnations Rama and Krishna (at noon on *Ramanavami* in April and at midnight on *Janmashthami* in August respectively). At Christmas time, Sathya Sai Baba's devotees in Coventry also sing carols to residents in a home for the elderly in accordance with Baba's exhortation to acts of community service.

As far as Christmas in schools is concerned, research in Coventry had no difficulty in finding that primary schools' preparations for Christmas included telling children the story of Jesus' birth in Bethlehem and how to make decorations to hang in their homes and greeting cards to give to their parents. In most schools there were rehearsals for an end of term event to which parents were invited. Equipped with an orange, a red ribbon, a pin, silver foil, four cocktail sticks and sweets or raisins, pupils also made Christingles (a Moravian custom imported into UK churches and schools from Slovakia in the late twentieth century).

Preparation for Christmas continues to dominate the autumn term, even in schools with a majority of pupils from non-Christian, South Asian families, although some schools have responded to demographic change. This was not the case in 1987 in a 99 per cent Asian first school in Southall, where the dominance of Christmas impelled the Muslim writer Yasmin Alibhai-Brown to write an eloquent polemic against 'A White Christmas'. Brown vehemently denounced 'the central power relationship where Christian social rites dominate ... behind the goodwill and expansiveness' and exposed the injustices of continuing colonialism.[7] Her outrage resonates with the exasperation and dismay of humanists, Jehovah's Witnesses and Jews.

The Coventry findings suggested that the presence of significant percentages of Hindu, Sikh and Muslim pupils in some schools, and teachers' growing awareness of a

need to introduce all children to cultural diversity, had helped to mould some Christmas-related events. By no means were all the plays that I watched nativity plays, and one school's presentation included, together with a Christmas play, a brief presentation of the Hindu festival of Divali and the Jewish celebration of Hanukkah. This was an affirmation of UK society's diverse faith traditions, rather than a response to local expectation, as no Jewish pupils attended the school.

By and large, however, schools' overwhelming emphasis on Christmas, and the lengthy preparations for special events, continued the experience of previous generations of British schoolchildren and promoted assumptions about the place of Christmas in the Christian tradition and in British culture that are shared by church leaders, churchgoers and Sunday school organisers.

As we have seen, it is true that families from many religious and cultural backgrounds do participate in secular aspects of the Christmas festivities. This increasingly shared practice provides an example of what the social anthropologist Gerd Baumann calls 'syncretisation by convergence'. In other words, faith communities A and B have absorbed practices which were previously characteristic of community C (the, socially most pervasive, Christian tradition). In many ways 'doing Christmas' (like having birthday parties and cake) makes children feel less different from their peers. It demonstrates not just the social pressure to conform to a perceived British norm but also many parents' will to conform, at least for the sake of their children. At the same time, as British Hindu Punjabi actress and author Meera Syal has suggested, in some ways 'joining in with the festivities is more a case of good manners than a gesture of solidarity'.[8]

Probably the two most powerful forces in this Christmas convergence are primary schools – with their presentation of a, for the most part, homogenised version of tradition – and television. Schools are not just teaching pupils about a tradition but, by the way that they process it and involve pupils of increasingly diverse backgrounds in it, are themselves transmitting and transforming tradition. And one of Christmas Day's principal activities – watching television with one's relatives – has brought a shared experience. Certainly for decades, schools and television have been the principal sources of information on Christmas for many Britons of South Asian background who seldom if ever visit a white Christian home – and are least likely to be invited on December 25th.

Eleanor Nesbitt

Knowing how we fail
our children's daily demands
we shower them with gifts.

Pat Pinsent

Chapter Nine
Giving Gifts

It is embedded in our assumptions about and expectations of Christmas that we give gifts. In recent years this has become a topic of much debate and interest as increasing numbers of people want to take a stand against Christmas becoming an ever more obscene display of conspicuous consumption in a world where so many want for the basics. The concept of 'ethical giving' has come to prominence, with charities encouraging us to buy a goat, a can of worms or a water tap – practical gifts which benefit communities of genuine need.

Why do we give gifts? What do they symbolise? We give gifts to those we love and care for as a sign of our affection and appreciation of them. And (ideally) gifts are given without hope of return, otherwise they cease truly to be gifts. In reality the giving of gifts at Christmas is often a more complex affair and many of us get caught up in our own and other people's expectations of what we/they think we should be giving or what we/they think is 'required' from our gift. It can be difficult to resist these pressures:

'Everyone in Navjeet's class wants the latest pair of trainers/newest gadget/toy this year. I don't want him to feel left out but money is tight. How can I help him understand that Christmas isn't just about acquiring the latest new fashion item? How will I feel if I don't buy him what he wants?'

'My wife's parents always get us things we don't really need or want. They mean well, I'm sure, but quite often what they give us ends up in a charity shop. How do I raise this issue with them without hurting their feelings?'

'I'd like to give an ethical gift to relatives this year – such as a sheep or school starter kit for people in a developing country. No one has done this before. Will they think I'm being mean – especially to the children?'

'There is so much encouragement to spend, spend, spend in the run-up to Christmas. I really hate that. It's just not what Christmas is about for me. Actually, I'd rather not give bought gifts this Christmas at all. What can I give instead?'

This chapter doesn't claim to offer easy answers to all these questions but we offer here various resources to help you think about gift-giving differently. Ultimately we all want the giving of gifts to be meaningful. What the pressure of Christmas gift buying can also reveal to us sometimes, however, is the quality of relationship we have (or don't have) with those for whom we are trying to find gifts ('I haven't a clue what Sally or Adam would like – I don't really know what they're into'). The painful cracks and fissures in familial relationships can be something we confront when we think about giving at this time of year. It may be difficult to raise the subject of Christmas gifts if you want to do them differently, but perhaps it's worth a try.

'God loves a cheerful giver' is a phrase we may know. Whether you're a believer or not, there is something in this saying about gift-giving being as much, if not more, about what it does for the giver as to the receiver. Many people take great pleasure in choosing the right gift for a loved one, and enjoy the anticipatory secrecy involved in wrapping and hiding presents. For some these things are as much part of what giving gifts is about as the excited chaos of ripped paper and squeals of delight on Christmas Day. Perhaps ultimately what matters is that we try to become more thoughtful in how and what we give, both to those who are close to us and in relation to the wider world in which we live.

Websites

Buy Nothing Christmas   www.buynothingchristmas.org

Originally started by Canadian Mennonites, Buy Nothing Christmas invites you to rummage around their website and 'join a movement dedicated to reviving the original meaning of Christmas giving'. Download their free information kit and posters, youth sessions and alternative gift ideas. Read founder Aiden Enns' statement on why he set up Buy Nothing and browse their further reading.

Alternatives for Simple Living   www.simpleliving.org

A non-profit organisation that equips people of faith to 'challenge consumerism, live justly and celebrate responsibly'. Originally set up in 1973 as a protest against the commercialisation of Christmas. Full of resources and ideas.

Reverend Billy and the Church of Stop Shopping   www.revbilly.com

The Reverend Billy and the Stop Shopping Gospel Choir believe that consumerism is overwhelming our lives. Whilst not specifically focused on Christmas, this New York City-based organisation engage in 'guerrilla theatrics' throughout the USA to challenge a corporate culture of consumption. Listen to the Beatitudes of Buylessness, or invite the Reverend Billy to your school, organisation or community.

Give an alternative gift

There are now lots of ways to give gifts where they are really needed via a whole raft of alternative gift charity websites and catalogues. Usually the giver receives a card and sometimes a little token extra like a cuddly toy, etc, and the gift goes to where it can make a genuine difference to the quality of an individual's or a community's life.

The Alternative Christmas List	www.thealternativechristmaslist.co.uk
Cafod	www.cafod.org.uk/worldgifts
Christian Aid	www.presentaid.org
Concern Worldwide	www.concerngifts.org
Crisis	www.crisispud.org.uk
Farm Friends	www.farmfriends.org.uk
Oxfam	www.oxfamunwrapped.com
Practical Action	www.practicalpresents.org
Send a Cow	www.sendacow.org.uk
Traidcraft	www.giftsforlife.org
World Vision	www.greatgifts.org

> Use newspaper, with articles and photos showing the good news about our world, as wrapping paper.
>
> *Kitty Price*

Ethical shopping

In the 21st century, those of us who consume more of the world's resources also have a responsibility to make informed choices about where and how we spend our money. Books such as *The Good Shopping Guide* (published by the Ethical Consumer Research Association) rate the world's major companies in ethical terms, checking out their track records on issues such as investment in arms, animal testing and environmental concern. 'Gooshing' is the term given to ethical shopping online as well as the name of a website which enables you to search for the most ethical products and best prices on a whole range of goods. For fair trade fashion and gorgeous gifts, support companies with clear and upfront ethical policies:

www.thegoodshoppingguide.co.uk
www.gooshing.co.uk
www.ethicalconsumer.org
www.shopethic.com
www.ethical-junction.org
www.greenshop.co.uk
www.naturalcollection.com
www.ganesha.co.uk
www.ptree.co.uk

Some doing it differently Christmas present and card ideas

🎄 With family and friends, agree on a limit to what you are going to spend. Send the rest to charity.

🎄 Decide with a group of friends or family that you are all going to spend no more than £2–£5 on each other. Have fun seeing what imaginative and unusual gifts you can discover for relatively small amounts of money. How far can you make it go?

🎄 Put all names of the family in a hat and then have everyone pick one (not their own). Everyone then buys and gives one present.

🎄 Give gifts to the kids but not to the adults. They'll cope.

🎄 Buy your gifts from charities.

🎄 Give fair trade goods.

🎄 Buy from independent local traders. Support your community!

🎄 If you're giving foodstuffs buy locally sourced products. This will mean less impact on the environment. Buy organic if you can. See **www.soilassociation. org/christmas**

🎄 Ask your friends and family what they want (and what they don't want).

🎄 Make your own gifts: biscuits, cakes, jams, poems, art, clothing, jewellery, accessories, etc.

🎄 With your children, make up a Christmas box for a child in a less privileged part of the world. See Samaritan's Purse **www.samaritanspurse.uk.com** and Mustard Seed **www.msrm.org**

🎄 Give gifts of time: offer to take someone to see a film, or for a meal, or to do something they'd really like to do. Give a massage voucher (or three!) or a voucher for a babysitting session.

🎄 Give a goat, etc – see 'Give an alternative gift', p.135.

🎄 Use the run-up to Christmas as a time for your children to consider which toys they no longer play with. Donate the toys to a charity shop – then there will be room for the new ones.

🎄 For wrapping paper, buy rolls of recycled paper and potato print it, or paint your own festive patterns.

🎄 Make your own Christmas cards: get creative with glitter, glue, metallic paints, gorgeous papers …

🎄 Recycle last year's Christmas cards to make this year's, or use them to make gift tags.

🎄 Send a Christmas card to a prisoner of conscience or human rights defender. Every year between November and January Amnesty International holds a Greetings Card Campaign. See **www.amnesty.org.uk** for further details.

🎄 Only send cards to people you don't see regularly. Give those you see all the time something of yourself, such as a warm Christmas greeting and a hug.

🎄 If Christmas 'round robins' make you cringe, chuckle over Simon Hoggart's *The Hamster That Loved Puccini: The Seven Modern Sins of Christmas Round Robin Letters* (Atlantic Books, 2005) and *The Cat That Could Open the Fridge: A Curmudgeon's Guide to Christmas Round Robin Letters* (Atlantic Books, 2004). These make great gifts.

I heard a story about a woman who asked all her friends to send her a candle for Christmas and the money they would have spent on presents to charity. She then had a roomful of candles reflecting the love of friends and family – and the knowledge that money had gone to those much more in need.

Jo Jones

Alternatives to buying

🎄 Arrange a toy swap in your area. Have children spruce up and wrap outgrown toys, books, games and sporting equipment for exchange.

🎄 Offer to paint a room, take care of the children, walk the dog, wash the windows, sew a dress, frame a picture, wire a lamp, cook the Christmas dinner … What else can you do for a friend?

🎄 Help a child to make candles, a pomander, a pin cushion, a pot holder, stuffed animals, puppets, scrapbooks and other gifts.

🎄 Organise a community celebration: a pot luck supper, lucky dip and songs. Decorate the room with handmade decorations.

🎄 Teach someone to play a musical instrument, bake a cake, enlarge a photograph.

Think of other skills you might share.

🎄 Remember prisoners, old people and children in care. Plan an outing or regular visits to cheer them up. Continue your interest after the holidays.

🎄 Create a poem or song or painting.

🎄 Borrow (from a library) books, DVDs or CDs a friend would enjoy.

🎄 Help a child to fix something broken. Show the child how to use such things as scissors, Sellotape, a hammer and nails, a needle and thread, to repair a toy, an item of clothing or a piece of furniture.

🎄 Share your car, boat, sewing machine, tools or garden with friends. You could give a corner of your garden as an allotment to an elderly neighbour. You could offer the use of your home for a party.

🎄 Cook Christmas foods with others. Invite friends round to share their family recipes – then the cooking can become part of the holiday festivities rather than a chore for one person. Homemade pies and cakes could be given as presents in hand-decorated boxes.

🎄 Sew a simple pattern, then personalise it with embroidered initials. Sew floor cushions, pillows, place mats or a rug to suit the recipient's taste. Make soft toys, beanbags or puppets for a child.

🎄 Renew an old possession: make new clothes for a well-loved doll, rebind a tattered book, revarnish a scarred chair or table.

🎄 Build shelves, a spice rack, a window box, a bird table, a gerbil cage, a sandbox, a doll's house, a set of toy blocks.

🎄 Plant bulbs to bloom in the middle of winter. Plant a windowsill herb garden.

From Pax Christi

A friend told me that she found, scattered across her garden, fir cones and seeds from the cones. Springing up in different places were seedling Christmas trees. So she has gathered up the seeds and will give them to friends for Christmas. My friend commented that she suddenly realised, as she saw the seeds, that here was the entire Christmas message of new life, death and resurrection.

Jo Jones

A Christmas 'Our Father'

Our Father,
which art in Dixons,
hallowed be thy games;
thy new releases come,
thy videoing be done,
in Nicam as it is in mono;
give us this day our daily emails,
and forgive us for not spending enough,
as we forgive those who spend too little on us;
lead us not into Oxfam,
but deliver us from charitable giving;
for thine is the DVD,
the widescreen and the Game Boy,
for ever and ever.
Amen

Rachel Mann

M£rry Chri$tmas

Dashing round the store
On a late December day,
Through the aisles we go,
Trolleys in the way.
Bells on tills go ring,
Making wallets light,
Oh, what fun to trek round town,
Now open late at night.

Jingle tills, jingle tills,
Profit all the way,
Oh, what fun it is to spend
Your overdraft away.
Jingle tills, jingle tills,
Profit all the way,
Oh, what fun it is to shop
On Jesus Christ's birthday.

Rebecca Warren

You shouldn't have

You shouldn't have given me those terrible socks.
I thought it was chocolates 'til I opened the box
and found the most hideous footwear I've seen.
I suppose they might suit me if I were fifteen,
with their acid house patterns and colours (Day-Glo);
I'm afraid after Christmas to Oxfam they'll go.
Really, you shouldn't have.

You shouldn't have sent me that car maintenance book.
I lifted the bonnet and risked a quick look:
it's all wires and knobs and sticking-out bits,
there's so much stuff I'm amazed it fits.
I'm afraid if I messed with it I wouldn't get far
and the next thing I'd know is I'd need a new car.
Really, you shouldn't have.

You shouldn't have sent me that shiny LP,
much smaller than usual and called a CD.
I knew something was wrong when the needle came down
and the speakers screamed to wake the whole town.
It must be that newfangled indy-grunge-pop –
whatever it's called, it's going back to the shop.
Really, you shouldn't have.

You shouldn't have spent so much on this hat:
it sits on my head like a giant cowpat,
and looks like a salad bowl filled full of fruit,
with a cherry on top and lettuce to boot!
If I went out with that on my head
I'm utterly sure I'd lose my street-cred.
Really, you shouldn't have.

You shouldn't have knitted that interesting scarf.
It's quite long (I measured it): a mile and a half!
I just got it off but needed some aid:
cut out by the local fire brigade.
Just so you don't think this letter's all gripes,
I'm using the pieces for lagging the pipes.
Really, you shouldn't have.

And is this all Christmas is really about:
useless presents we could well do without?
Grumbles when we get what we don't really want
and have to say thank you to some boring aunt?
If that's all it's for and that's how it is,
we might as well give up, admit it's a swizz.
You shouldn't have. Really, you shouldn't have.

But for all of the handkerchiefs, bath salts and soap,
there's something about Christmas, something about hope,
and a birth in a manger, a child in a stable
far from the shops and the over-full table,
where God came among us from heaven above
and showed in that giving astonishing love.
He shouldn't have.

He shouldn't have gone through all that for us –
the birth, the humility, the death on a cross –
yet he did, and everything's changed by that life,
bringing light out of darkness, peace out of strife.
He emptied himself in love beyond measure,
so that life in its fullness and all heaven's treasure
we should have.

Tony McClelland

Resisting the power of the marketplace
(from the Tikkun Community)

The loss of the heart of the spiritual message of Christmas – its subversion into a frenetic orgy of consumption – rightly disturbs Christians and other people of faith. But this transformation is not a result of Jewish or Muslim parents wanting to protect their children from being forced to sing Christmas carols in school, or of secularists sending 'Season's Greetings' cards. It derives instead from the power of the capitalist marketplace, operating through television, movies and marketers, to drum into everyone's mind the notion that the only way to be a decent human being at this time of year is to buy more and more. Thus the altruistic instinct to give, which could take the form of giving of our time, our skills and our loving energies to people we care about, gets degraded into a competitive whirlwind of spending.

In the Network of Spiritual Progressives, an interfaith project of the Tikkun Community **(www.spiritualprogressives.org)**, we have done what we could: we've organised a series of informational picketing events at major shopping centres and distributed our message about ethical consumption for the holiday season. We particularly emphasised giving gifts of time instead of giving gifts of things.

Friends and neighbours get a card saying: 'I promise you five hours of help mowing your grass', 'shovelling your snow', 'providing child care so you can go out', 'teaching your children a sport or sharing some talent I have' (e.g. music, computer, language lessons), 'helping you with shopping or with cleaning or cooking'. (There are endless possibilities here, depending on the needs of the person to whom you are giving the gift.)

We understand that many people feel inadequate during the Christmas season precisely because they don't have enough money to buy the kinds of gifts that their friends and children are being taught (by the media) to be the sine qua non of 'really caring'. So people are disappointed as they stand with the Christmas tree or Chanukah menorah and find that the gifts they received don't measure up to the marketplace-induced fantasies. Meanwhile, the spiritual message of the holidays gets largely lost. No wonder people feel distraught. Our task is to help them understand that the solution is not in blaming secular people, civil libertarians, Jews, Muslims, or anyone else for this sense of loss, but instead in recognising that the emptiness or feeling of loneliness or lack has been forced upon them by market values that they need to become aware of so they can then reject them.

Rabbi Michael Lerner

Advent friends
(from L'Arche Edinburgh)

In the ecumenical community we are part of – the L'Arche Community in Edinburgh – we celebrate the custom of 'Advent friends'. The community has a dispersed membership of some fifty people, including people with learning disabilities who live in two houses that are shared with assistants, and numerous other people, employed and volunteers, who live in the local area and are involved in many different ways. Not everyone knows everyone else equally well. Some people have joined the community recently; some have been part of it for many years.

At the start of Advent, during community prayer, each person draws out of a bowl the name of someone else. If you pick your own name you put it back. A visitor for the day compiles a discreet list of who has who, in case there is any need to refer to it later on. The name drawn is your Advent friend. You keep it secret all through Advent until a final time of gathering and prayer just before Christmas Day. During the season I will remember my Advent friend in a special way, sending them little gifts (such as homemade biscuits) and cards anonymously, and praying for them. Unexpected surprises arrive through the post, or get dropped off mysteriously during the evenings, causing great excitement. People disguise their handwriting, or write with their non-writing hand.

If my Advent friend is someone I do not know then I ask their friends for ideas about what to make or buy them as a Christmas present for the final gathering. A limit is set as to what to spend on this gift – £7–£8. Finally, everyone comes together just before Christmas and, after a wee mime of the Bethlehem story, the first gift is unwrapped. The only thing the gifts have written on them is the name of the recipient. Everyone has time for one guess as to who has been giving to them throughout Advent – only one guess, mind! The giver then reveals him/herself.

As well as being a fun way to celebrate waiting, this tradition also ensures that each person who is part of the group is given one gift, and only one gift, from the group with whom they have shared the last year.

Anthony and Magnus Kramers

Giving gifts at Cropthorne

We had agreed at the start of our Cropthorne Christmas how we would 'do presents': we were each given a small paper 'present bag' – the kind you can buy at stationery and gift card shops – and then we put all our names into a hat and picked out one each. That was the person whose present bag we would be filling. In addition, we set a £1 limit on what we would each spend. We had two days in which to try to think as imaginatively and creatively as possible about what we could buy – or find, or make – for our designated person. This was great fun. In our immediate vicinity the only shop was a post office/general store, but yet another restraint on what we could actually buy only added to the challenge – and fun.

How far does £1 go? Remarkably far when you set your mind to it and every penny counts! The most luxurious gift that any of us gave was a hand-sewn scarf made of silky, shiny gold material from a haberdasher's in Pershore (precisely one pound's worth!). Other presents we bought were more ordinary – travel tissues, a comb, sweets – but hopefully useful or small treats. Some of us also made or wrote things: one person gave a poem.

These gifts were given on Christmas Day, after lunch, as part of the 'Liturgy of the gifts' (see Chapter 11). We took turns opening our present bags, so everyone enjoyed each person's receiving of their gifts. We also tried to guess who had been our 'Secret Santa'. I remember this present-giving as a relaxed time – after all we'd just had our Christmas dinner!; and the gift-giving also came symbolically at the end of the liturgical journey that the group had made together. We had created a different way of doing Christmas together, and our gifts were also an expression of thanks and appreciation for the people who had made that journey with us.

Rosie Miles

This year we are giving 'time' to some members of the family: a weekend looking after the children. To local friends whom we don't see often enough we are giving a 'meal voucher' for them to come over and spend an evening with us.

Jo Rathbone

Sharing the chocolate

Last Christmas was particularly poignant for me, as a young girl whom I had been supporting with a little friendship – an asylum-seeker from Sierra Leone – disappeared from the address I had for her about ten days before Christmas. This girl had been suicidal a few months previously and although still on medication she had started attending a church, singing in the choir and had proudly begun a college course. On further enquiry we discovered that she had been moved about sixty miles away to another town. I tried to find a church that would welcome her there but emails were not replied to and the people to whom I spoke claimed either not to know her address or that they were new to the area themselves. I'd hoped in vain that a church would offer to collect her for the Christmas service and maybe even invite her for lunch, but it was not to be. Definitely no room at the inn! I took a very small box of chocolates to the Post Office for her with two days to go only to be told by the postmistress that 'it won't get there *now*, you know'.

However, on Christmas night she phoned me as I was driving and I stopped to take the call. It was snowing and I wept as she told me that my present *had* arrived on Christmas Eve. She was living in a hostel with four women who had been quite cold towards her up until now; but sharing the chocolate – the only present that they had between all of them – had broken the ice and they had all sat together and prayed. I was humbled and felt that here was the true spirit of Christmas.

Agnes

Christmas cards and presents: to do or not to do?

The most important thing here for me is communication. So many people I have talked with about Christmas say they *want* to do it differently, but don't want to offend or look mean. So I have found that telling people what is going on is the most helpful thing. It's like the emperor's new clothes. Everyone seems to agree that Christmas has got too commercial and it's a pressure. No one wants to play the game – but everyone thinks they have to. Learning to do it differently takes courage.

So keep it simple. Be honest. Talk to your friends, and make agreements about what you're sending or giving each other. I believe it's okay to set limits, but also to acknowledge what is expected by those much older or younger than me. For example, I will definitely send cards and letters to grandad and my godparents, whom I see infrequently and who I know would be offended at not receiving a card. Similarly, I will buy gifts for my nieces and nephews, but not necessarily for their parents. I may give some cards to my neighbours in the spirit of neighbourliness, but I don't hand cards to my friends or colleagues: I wish them a happy Christmas instead.

Last year, we agreed among a small group of friends that we would not spend more than a fiver on each other. One friend sent the money she would have spent to Christian Aid, which we all thought was a great idea. Most of the people I know say they have too much clutter rather than too little. Few of us actually *need* the presents we receive at Christmas.

I have also learnt from seriously ill people how to do Christmas differently. A friend with severe ME/Chronic Fatigue buys all her gifts from catalogues. So last year my partner and I chose a charity catalogue and spent two hours at the kitchen table one Saturday afternoon 'going shopping'. It did mean that some of the presents were very slightly odd, but it was easily the least stressful experience of Christmas shopping either of us had ever had, and one we will definitely be repeating this year.

Gaynor Harper

Chapter Ten
Practical Suggestions

This chapter contains a variety of practical ideas to help us think about the entire season of Christmas, from its start at the beginning of Advent, through to its conclusion at Candlemas. Most of the suggestions focus on December itself. How do we claim a sense of our own rhythms at this time of year – not to mention those of the depths of winter itself – amidst the relentless build-up to the 'big day'? As well as thoughts on how we might look after ourselves better – body, mind and spirit – throughout Christmas, you will also find many ideas here which invite us to include and welcome others into our Christmas preparations and festivities.

Some principles and guidelines for doing December differently

These guidelines range from small-scale, individual choices to larger theological and liturgical themes that might underlie a church's approach to Christmas. Both seem important in attempting to find a way of doing December differently.

Do what you can to make small changes. There is always the option of making some kind of change which can shift things, however small it may seem. Do not despair! Refuse to feel trapped.

Be compassionate – to yourself as well as to your relations, friends, parishioners, etc. Be as gentle with yourself as it's possible to be, and be realistic about what you can and can't expect to 'get out' of Christmas. Give up the illusion of the 'perfect Christmas'. Weave the wounds and flaws into the cloth.

Cherish and claim limitation, restraint, simplicity and 'enough-ness' as sound Advent principles, inasmuch as you can. Practise saying no. Stay in. Create small spaces for silence, rest, prayer, in whatever ways you can manage amidst the mayhem.

Plan ahead. Write yourself a note during or just after *this* Christmas to remind yourself of the things you need to remember next year. Stick it in your diary for sometime around the middle of November.

Communicate. Talk to family and friends about how you plan to, or would prefer to, manage Christmas. Explain what you are going to do and why. Expect them to understand; but even if they don't, be clear and consistent.

Make connections with people and places very different from yourself and your own context. Find some ways, however small-scale, of welcoming the stranger in your midst. This may be on your doorstep or on the other side of the world. Utilise links with charities and churches in other parts of the world to extend hospitality and concern to those who need prayer and/or material support. Assist the poor and marginalised in your own neighbourhood or city, or, at the very least, bring their names and stories into your liturgies, preaching, prayer, thoughts.

Reclaim the liturgy. For Christians the liturgical calendar is one of the strongest weapons against the trivialisation and exploitation of Christmas. Advent, with its themes of judgment, death, heaven and hell, as well as its ascetic dimensions, provides fantastic opportunities for exploring sombre realities in our world, as well as a framework to encourage and reclaim restraint and a right simplicity in a greedy, consumerist society. Christmas itself, with its themes of incarnation, God's compassion for the poor and marginalised, the overturning of the expectations of the mighty and learned, the welcome to the stranger, etc, is ripe for exploration in all kinds of counter-cultural ways. The saints' days surrounding Christmas (e.g. Stephen's, Holy Innocents') are stark reminders of the reality of violence woven into the Christmas story and cut against sentimentalism and cosy domesticity. Epiphany, with its emphasis on the 'appearing' of Christ, celebrates the insights of those from other lands (the Magi), and links the birth of Christ with the beginning of his public ministry at his baptism and at Cana – lots of possibilities here to get away from idolisation of the infant.

Reclaim the positive yet critical engagement with culture from which the original celebration of Christmas emerged. Whichever tradition explaining the origins of the festival of Christmas we opt for (see Chapter 8), it seems clear that the ancient Church's celebration of the birth of Christ on December 25th was a robust way of engaging with their culture and challenging some of its most prevalent values and assumptions. Advent developed as an alternative to the pagan festival of Saturnalia which was marked by excess and debauchery. Christmas may have developed as an alternative to the winter solstice, proclaiming Jesus as the 'Sun of righteousness' who outshines all the pagan gods. In what ways can we celebrate Christmas today so that we engage with culture yet also contest its hedonism, narcissism and myopia? This might be a good theme for an Advent sermon or study group.

Try to keep a sense of perspective. It will pass! Build in good recovery time afterwards. Give up on guilt. Laugh at the god-awful bits. Cherish the unexpected moments of wonder.

Nicola Slee

Advent tea

My family has always enjoyed marking the seasons and celebrating key events in the cycle of nature, the liturgical year and folk tradition. One of our regular events is what we call Advent tea.

Tea times on the four Sundays of Advent offer opportunities for entertaining people one would not normally invite for a meal. Towards the end of November we begin to ask each other whom we want to invite to tea on each of the four Advent Sundays. We aim for a spread of ages, and are careful to include each week someone elderly (particularly if they might be lonely), someone single and a family with young children. In theory the invitations can be extended to Christmas Eve for the lighting of the fifth candle, but quite often we are too disorganised for that, so the final event of the sequence is just celebrated as a family.

The main pattern of events for each tea is:

> saying grace, if appropriate
> a reading
> the lighting of the candle(s)
> eating and conversation
> the extinguishing of the candle(s)

The oldest person present is invited to do the reading, and the youngest lights the candle(s). Special words can be said when lighting the candle(s), but this is optional. At the end of the meal the candle(s) can be blown out by another child, while in our imaginations we all send the light to people we care about: hungry children, someone who is ill, a lonely relative far away, a country at war ...

The whole ritual is infinitely flexible. If all the guests are Christians, the reading might be one of the pre-Christmas Bible readings such as Isaiah's prophecy (Isaiah 7:10–14) or the Annunciation story (Luke 1: 26–38); or a poem or reflective piece of prose can be used instead. If few or none of the guests are Christian, the grace can be dropped and the readings can be entirely secular – although we still try to preserve the Advent sense of waiting. With guests from other reli-

gious traditions, the reading might be from one of their sacred books.

This is the only time of the year when we sit down to afternoon tea, so we make a special effort by setting the table attractively, having fresh flowers and providing simple but appetising food.

Things you will need

A candleholder and five candles. Years ago we cut a log in half lengthways, drilled holes in it with an augur – four in a circle and one in the middle – and rubbed linseed oil into the wood. This homemade candle log comes out each year and is very much a part of the tradition for us, but obviously any candleholder can be used. The log is decorated with green leaves, red berries and cones; and if there are any small flowers in bloom, these are added. The outer candles are white and the central candle is red, or for a change the outer ones could be green and the central one could be purple. Each week an additional candle is lit, culminating in the central candle on the Sunday before Christmas.

Guests

Four to eight guests, depending on the size of the host family or community. There should not be too many to sit comfortably round the table.

Food

This depends on the culture and tastes of the hosts. In planning the event, however, it should be remembered that this is a Sunday afternoon tea, not a smart dinner party: the idea is not to spend time and money on lavish entertainment, but to share the good things of the household and to get to know each other better. A typical spread in our home would include vegetarian pâtés, cheese and pickle, celery and baby tomatoes, followed by cake, fruit and crumpets with honey or homemade jam. Children tend to like some biscuits and juice; squash or milk is provided for them while the adults drink tea.

We have kept Advent teas simple and uncomplicated, because that's the only way to ensure that we get round to doing it every year. Few people experience a sit-down Sunday tea these days, so guests enjoy it and tend to remember it as a special treat.

Alwyn Marriage

Make the most of Advent
(some ideas for children)

Celebrate Stir-up Sunday. This is the Sunday before Advent starts (the fifth Sunday before Christmas). It is the traditional time for stirring your Christmas pudding. The name comes from the collect in the *Book of Common Prayer* which begins, 'Stir up, O Lord, the wills of your people …' and the day is about preparing spiritually for Christmas. Use it as a time to gather the household around the kitchen table, stir your puddings and talk about your hopes for the coming season.

Go to an Advent carol service. This is more of a grown-up activity, as Advent carols do tend to be more reflective and sombre than Christmas ones – but do not assume that children will not respond to the haunting music and beauty of the Advent liturgy. Cathedrals and city churches are good places to search out an Advent carol service. Radio 4 broadcasts a service live from one of the Cambridge colleges. If listening at home, you could light candles and reflect on the readings and music. Or you could do your own shortened, simplified version.

Take part in the posada. This is a Latin American tradition which, as a community, we have adapted to our circumstances. During Advent we remember the journey of Mary and Joseph to Bethlehem. In Spain, a couple spends Advent going from house to house asking for hospitality. However, we British aren't so good at giving hospitality (especially unexpectedly and to strangers), so we use the crib figures of Mary, Joseph and the donkey. Each day during Advent the figures 'stay' with someone different in the community. When they arrive there is a brief ceremony in which people use this symbolic journey to help them recall all those who travel or who are far from home, including refugees and other homeless people. The posada liturgy asks the question: 'Is there room in *your* heart and at your hearth for the Christchild?' Forms of the posada liturgy are available from a number of places, including the Church Army's website **(www.churcharmy.org.uk)**. Why not get together with friends and use the liturgy as an opportunity to anticipate Christmas together? Or use it as an opportunity to get to know someone better.

Make a Jesse tree. Up until the Reformation many churches had a Jesse tree. The Jesse tree is a symbolic representation of the ancestors of Christ, a kind of family tree of Jesus. The idea comes from Isaiah 11:1: 'A shoot will spring forth from the stump of Jesse, and a branch out of his roots.' Jesse was the father of David, and Jesus was from the line of David. Jesse trees are made using a 'dead' twiggy branch. This is to contrast with the green tree we use at Christmas, which symbolises that in Jesus we have eternal life. The two trees also symbolise the old covenant and the new covenant (although contemporary Christians will need to take care about perpetuat-

ing negative and stereotypical understandings of Judaism as 'the old covenant'). The decorations hung on the Jesse tree, therefore, are all reminiscent of the Old Testament. Examples are an apple, fig leaf, or snake for Adam and Eve; an ark, dove, or rainbow for Noah; stars for Abraham; a ladder (possibly with an angel) for Jacob; a multi-coloured coat for Joseph; a lion for Daniel ... Traditionally, the symbols placed on the Jesse tree have tended to be derived from male characters. There is every reason for widening this out to include women from the Jewish scriptures, as indeed Matthew's genealogy (Matthew 1) does. When we first started this custom we used our *Lion Children's Bible* to give us ideas; it became our bedtime storybook for Advent. As Advent wore on we added things we made. You can also add purple things, as purple is the colour of Advent. Having a Jesse tree also means that you can delay setting up your Christmas tree!

Light an Advent candle at mealtimes. It does not need to be one with numbers on it – any candle will do. If you are really ambitious you could make an Advent wreath with four candles. The candles are usually red, or three purple and one pink. (The pink one is for Mary and is lit at the beginning of the week before Christmas.) Begin lighting candles on Advent Sunday.

Celebrate Saint Nicholas's Day (December 6th). Saint Nicholas was a bishop in Turkey (Myra) in the fourth century AD. He is the patron saint of children (because he resurrected some boys who had been dismembered by a butcher) and spinsters (he anonymously gave bags of gold to three sisters who did not have dowries). In our home St Nicholas mysteriously delivers a bag of golden chocolate coins to each child on the night of December 5th. In Germany, it is customary to have 'St Nicholas gingerbread'. (We use a gingerbread lady biscuit-cutter and then give each figure a triangular 'hat' for a bishop's mitre.)

Set up your nativity scene but ... only set up the stable. Place the people, etc around the room. Mary, Joseph and the donkey could move a little closer to the stable each day, arriving Christmas Eve. Put Jesus in the stable after the children's bedtime. The shepherds could tend their sheep on a 'hillside' somewhere. The Magi could be placed farther away, and not begin their journey to the stable until after Christmas Day. They arrive on January 6th.

Jane Still

A winter solstice celebration

As I have never embraced Christianity, I've always found this time of year a bit difficult. (As a pre-WW2 baby I grew up through fairly hard times and Christmas was an oh-so-needed landmark in the year. There was excitement and surprise, with parents doing unexpected things like hanging up paper chains, putting silver three-penny pieces in puddings and cursing over fairy lights that would never work, but which looked nice to me anyhow. There were little presents and new jumpers from aunties. And the grown-ups even drank a teensy bit of alcohol! So I look back on this period with nostalgia and I think my own children loved Christmas similarly.)

For me the nativity has a historical significance and that is all. And Christmas today has been built up into a monster of greed and commercial opportunism with people beggaring themselves to provide what is 'expected'. So I finally decided to turn my back on the whole shemozzle … But being a grandma to ten has its responsibilities and being a miserable old git isn't an option. So I have reverted to good old astronomical and biological ideas and have a winter solstice party for family, friends and neighbours.

The cause for celebration is simple: the passing of the shortest day and longest night with the hope of a new year of growth and rebirth. The wheel turns for a seasonal change and I can rejoice in the gentle movement from the dark, cold winter to the light, sweet spring, as well as create an opportunity to thank all those around who love and care for me.

So what happens? The children (supervised) are allowed to light outdoor fires. We have fireworks, sparklers, nightlights in jars, wood gathering and chopping. Then the children also light and keep fed my two open fires indoors. The house is mostly candlelit. In the kitchen everyone can make sun, moon and star cakes – fairy cakes with icing and silver and orange decorations. My guests make solstice cards with gold and silver cut-and-stick. They can make willow weavings with branches from my tree. Each child has a gold and silver bag containing gifts. Weather permitting, these are hung up on a tree outside. The gifts include a small torch, a piece of jewellery or a toy, a gold or silver decoration and a sweet of some kind. With the torches they then do a treasure hunt in the dark, finding things tucked up in odd places. Indoors we have another treasure hunt right through the house. I make pheasant soup and a veggie alternative; and we have cold meats, cheese, bean salad and other tasty bits and pieces, with a sun and moon cake for dessert.

My winter solstice celebration comes a week before most people start celebrating and has enough darkness, difference, scariness, wonder and danger attached to it to please both the children and the adults.

Yvonne Peecock

> To enable our children to understand that
> Christmas is not about 'family' but about
> being inclusive, we have invited people
> who otherwise might have been on their
> own, or who are a long way from home,
> to share it with us – such as foreign students
> at the local university and people working
> in this country to support their families
> back home.
>
> *Jo Rathbone*

DIY Christmas decorations

- Gather pine cones and spray or paint them gold and silver.
- Use coloured strips of recycled or unwanted paper to make paper chains.
- Have a 'decorations party' one Saturday or Sunday in December: invite your friends around and have fun with glitter, glue, cardboard, pipe cleaners, foil, metallic paints, etc.
- See who can create the most beautiful/outrageously camp fairy for the top of the tree.
- If you want to buy decorations then buy fair trade via Traidcraft, Tearcraft or Oxfam.
- Alternatively, purchase hand-crafted decorations from artists/craftspeople.
- If you travel abroad, collect decorations from different parts of the world. Use them as reminders of your travels and the people you met.

Rosie Miles

A tree with roots

Six million Christmas trees are bought in the UK alone each year and most are thrown out afterwards. Do you *really* need a real Christmas tree in your house? If so, buy one from a sustainable source and recycle it afterwards through your local authority. For trees certified by the Soil Association or the Forest Stewardship Council see **www.soilassociation.org/christmas** Alternatively, buy a tree that has roots, use it over Christmas, then replant it in your garden.

Annie Porthouse

A creative December workshop

The aim of this workshop is to offer time and space for people to reflect on their own feelings and attitudes towards Christmas and to explore and express them in a creative medium (e.g. writing, artwork, role play, mime, dance, etc). If appropriate, the workshop could also be used as a means of creating a shared liturgy.

Some starting points for writing and/or artwork:

🎄 Work with your loves and hates in relation to Christmas. Make a list of each, and turn this into a litany or a colourful collage of words and images.

🎄 Choose one particular Christmas – one that you remember as a very happy or painful time. Write in the first person about that experience. Or find colours and images that represent that experience.

🎄 Think of the individuals or groups in your community or parish who are most marginalised. Write or draw something that explores what Christmas might be like for them, either putting yourself in their shoes or addressing them on behalf of your community. Or write a litany for all those marginalised by Christmas.

🎄 Write a letter to your parents or children or other family members describing the kind of Christmas you would really like to have. Invite them to share it with you, or tell them why you would choose to do it without them. Or create an image of an inclusive family Christmas.

🎄 Imagine Christa born as a girl, either in our time or some other. Write or paint a piece exploring this.

🎄 Imagine the Magi as a group of wise women visiting the Christchild to pay homage. What gifts do they/we bring? Write or draw a piece exploring this.

🎄 Choose a popular carol and write your own words for it, reflecting your own experience and feelings around Christmas.

🎄 Write a manifesto for yourself stating the things you will do this year to make Christmas more authentic – or maybe just more bearable! Begin each line: 'This Christmas, I will ...' Or create an image that will remind you of the values you want to keep at the heart of Christmas.

Nicola Slee

Enjoy being alone on Christmas Day

Create your own rituals. If curling up in front of the television with the cat or dog is what you like doing then do it and don't feel guilty. If there's nothing on TV watch your favourite film.

Make yourself a special meal. You are worth it. Have wine or whatever you enjoy and celebrate with your favourite music, candles and memories.

Go for a long walk. Savour the sights and sounds and smells at your own pace.

Remember the 'santons'. French nativity scenes feature santons: figures of ordinary folk such as the butcher, the baker, etc. *All* are welcome at the stable, including you.

Don't resist your memories. We nearly all miss someone at Christmas – either because of happy associations, or because of the intensity of the 'happy families' message which is promoted. Accept the losses. Light a candle for those you miss – or drink a toast! Welcome the ghosts.

Volunteer at the local drop-in centre or similar and help other people have a good time at Christmas.

And finally … don't buy all that stuff about happy families and the cosy Christmas closeness that you are supposedly missing. You know it's not true.

Rowena Edlin White

Savouring the big day

In our house we don't make feasting the main focus of our Christmas Day. Instead of a huge turkey (that takes all morning to prepare, removing a frazzled cook from the fun) we pick our favourite meal (currently toad-in-the-hole) and make it together as a family – children and adults.

These things mean we have time to go to church, relish the unwrapping of presents, do something outside (there is always an outside toy) and actually enjoy the day for which it has taken so long to prepare. We also open one present at a time, encouraging the children to savour and play with their gifts rather than just open them wildly and then wonder what is going to happen next. Often the thing the children enjoy most costs little or nothing: last year it was walking round our neighbourhood looking at the Christmas lights.

Judith Nathanail

As part of our lifestyle we follow the 'LOAF principles': we buy food that is Locally produced, Organically grown, Animal friendly and Fairly traded. We aim to eat food that is simpler, less that is processed – food that takes time to prepare rather than being instant. For someone for whom this is new perhaps Advent and Christmas could be a good time to begin exploring.

Jo Rathbone

Celebrate the twelve days of Christmas
(some ideas for children)

Make the presents last. The first day of Christmas is December 25th and the last is January 5th. Ever since our children were about four and two years old we have kept back a number of presents for them to open from the second to the twelfth day of Christmas. So, on Christmas Day they open stockings and maybe three presents. This means that they actually play with their toys. This also avoids that awful moment when all the presents have been opened, the children are still in frantic 'feeding frenzy' mode and there are angry pouts or tears because there's nothing left. It avoids that awful anticlimactic feeling on Christmas afternoon. It also gives you a chance to write thank yous as you go along, a chance to get bargains in the sales and a chance to redeem yourself if you forgot to buy a desperately wanted item!

Try to think of special things to do over the twelve days. Think in terms of 'on the fourth day of Christmas we went to Auntie Flo's house' and so on. Make each day different. Keep a Christmas diary of what you did.

Take part in 'the journey of the Magi'. This ceremony is similar to the posada liturgy but is adapted from a German custom. Crib figures of the Magi 'travel' around a parish or community and visit different homes. The Magi symbolise the spiritual journey and the recognition of the significance of Jesus Christ in our lives. At the end of each visit, a blessing is said as someone inscribes (in chalk) the year (e.g. 2006) and the initials of the wise men by the door. Their initials 'C' (Caspar), 'M' (Melchior), 'B' (Balthazzar) stand for 'Christ bless this house' in Latin.[9]

Celebrate the twelfth day of Christmas (January 5th). We have a special wassail, in which we symbolically drive away 'evil spirits'. In the countryside a shotgun is fired through a tree's branches, and we set off a firework. Then we bless the apple tree which symbolises the source of food for us. We ask God to tend us as we tend the apple tree. We drink hot mulled cider and 'toast' the tree. Finally we go inside and partake of more mulled cider and a variety of Epiphany cakes (there are a number of recipes from all over Europe). It is common in the Judaeo-Christian tradition to mark the beginning of a day from when the sun goes down. So although January 5th is the twelfth day, from sundown it is also the first day of the season of Epiphany.[10]

Jane Still

The Twelfth Night group

Many years ago a woman living in a large city had a lousy Christmas. She thought that there must be other people who had a similar experience and so she placed an advertisement in a local paper, inviting like-minded people to meet in a central hotel on Twelfth Night. A number of people came along and the group became established, meeting at regular intervals. Periodically members would host evenings in their homes and there were trips to various places. The people who came to the group were divorced, separated or had never married. Some people did form partnerships, but more widely the group fostered numerous friendships, which continued to exist for many years.

Sybil Harvey-Lago

Make the most of Epiphany

(some ideas for children)

Use your nativity scene. Place the figures of the wise men at a distance from the nativity scene at the beginning of Christmas (e.g. in another room). Move the figures closer and closer to the nativity scene through the twelve days of Christmas; have them 'arrive' at the stable on Epiphany. Move them there before the children come down in the morning and leave the children a gift from the wise men. In our house the wise men usually bring something that looks exotic, like an oriental fan or a carved wooden box.

Take down the Christmas decorations together. I know households that keep some decorations up all through the season of Epiphany. I try to keep the nativity scene out until Candlemas (February 2nd), which marks the end of Epiphany and celebrates the presentation in the Temple of Jesus by his parents. (Luke 2:22–38)

Jane Still

ALTERnativity   www.alternativity.org.uk

ALTERnativity aims to encourage people within the church and in the community to:

⚘ Look again at the celebration of Christmas and Advent in relation to environmental, economic and social issues.

⚘ Make their own choices and not to be dominated by external forces (such as media, advertising or tradition) if it is not what they want.

⚘ Focus on Advent economics as expressed in the Magnificat.

⚘ Work together to make the changes they want.

ALTERnativity offers worship resources which relate to the global context (where 30,000 people die daily from poverty)

Contact ALTERnativity c/o Christian Aid Scotland, 759a Argyle Street, Glasgow, G3 8DS, Scotland, United Kingdom

Part Three

Liturgical and Ritual Resources

Chapter Eleven
Coming In from the Cold

This chapter contains rites, reflections and liturgies that welcome those who have felt disenfranchised from Christmas, for whatever reasons. For us, this chapter is the pulsing heart of the book. The five liturgies that we undertook and created for our Cropthorne Christmas are given here, in the order in which we journeyed through them. We hope that they will provide inspiration and ideas for others who want to attempt their own alternative Christmas; they can, of course, be adapted to fit groups or situations.

Wrapping up our hurts
Cropthorne liturgy 1

This liturgy was designed to deal with negative images of Christmas. Prior to worship we made a list of what we loved and hated about Christmas (see Introduction), which we drew upon here.

Preparation

You will need: pens, paper, matches, a metal tray, and bed sheets or long strips of cloth (one for each person present). The bed sheets/strips of cloth are twisted into lengths and laid out in a 'star' formation in the middle of the gathering space (the ends of the sheets in the centre of the star are laid on top of each other). The participants sit in a spacious circle, around the sheets.

The liturgy has three parts:

Denunciation

Participants write on pieces of paper the things they hate/dislike about Christmas. If you have had a prior brainstorm on this subject use that, or people may want to add additional personal and private thoughts. Place the hates/dislikes in the metal tray and consign them to flames.

Affirmation

Prior to gathering, participants are asked to bring to the liturgy a personal object/ article/token (e.g. an inspirational poem or book, a trinket with particular individual value) that signifies for them how they have dared to think differently – at Christmas and/or at other times as well. During the affirmation people place these in the centre of the gathering space, and offer a word or two about the significance of their item if they wish.

Wrapping up our hurts

Participants take it in turn (probably in silence) gently to fold up a sheet around the centre 'meeting point' of all the sheets, as a way of binding up the wounds of bad experiences (not necessarily exclusively of Christmas). Once those past hurts have been bound up they can be safely left, while the group/community finds its own ways of celebrating.

The wrapped up sheets also produce an image of swaddling clothes which could be used in another liturgy – perhaps on Christmas Day – if you are planning a series/sequence of liturgies. The National Theatre production of the mystery plays

some years ago used such an image to spectacular effect when a bundle of rags was dramatically unfurled at the point of the birth of the Christchild.

During the Cropthorne Christmas the wrapped up bundle was taken into the chapel and left there for the remainder of our time together. It was quietly and privately unravelled at the end of our week, although this unravelling could be given its own ritual if that seems appropriate for the group.

Peter Kettle

A liturgy of friendship
Cropthorne liturgy 2

Background

For many of us who gathered at Cropthorne for Christmas, friends constitute our primary community. We were mostly single and/or lesbian and gay, for whom conventional nuclear family ties were sometimes problematic and for whom friends are particularly important in offering the support and community which we may not receive from partners, children or family.

Whilst friendship has an ongoing significance for us all year round it takes on a particular resonance at Christmas, when we are in touch with many people who have been important to us at some stage of our lives via cards, letters and emails. We were also friends together during our residential week. Some of us knew several others in the group; others knew only one or two. There were many overlapping friendship ties which constituted the group before we began and others were created as the week progressed. This liturgy, then, was created out of the living friendship of members of the gathered group, and offered a space to explore an aspect of our lives which is of deep and central importance.

This liturgy of friendship focuses on the story of Mary going to visit her cousin Elizabeth after her encounter with the angel (the Visitation). The meeting between the two women is seen as a paradigm of friendship. Around this central story we reflected on our own experiences of friendship and named the friends who are important to us.

The liturgy has five sections, after a brief introduction setting the theme: Mary's journey to Elizabeth; the meeting between the two women; a more general reflection on friendship; a naming and affirming of friends; a closing meditation on interdependence.

Resources

A number of visual images of the Visitation were used as a key part of the reflection, as well as readings on friendship. Images can be readily found in art books or by doing a Google Image search under 'Visitation'. A circle dance was also used.

Introduction

The leader introduces the liturgy with the following, or other suitable words:

Leader: We have journeyed to this place from many different settings and concerns. We have greeted one another and renewed or formed friendship. In this liturgy we take time to journey towards a deeper understanding of friendship and a celebration of its significance in our lives.

Mary's journey

Leader: 'In those days Mary set out and went with haste to a Judean town in the hill country ...'
Mary journeys alone to her cousin Elizabeth.
Mary journeys with a mysterious, terrifying secret in her soul.
How does Mary journey? In fear? In terror? In awe? In confusion?

Our journeys both to and within this place may be
    lonely and shared;
    fearful and joyful;
    confusing and comforting.

We take time now to journey on our own, to reflect on where we are on our Christmas journey, and then to regather and greet each other in peace.

The leader sends the group out into the available space – outside as well, if possible – to journey alone and in silence for a specified time (say 5–10 minutes).

Mary and Elizabeth meet

As individuals gather back at a specified location, they greet each other with a sign of peace. Then a greetings dance is performed. At the end of the dance the group gathers in a circle.

A reflection on friendship

Leader: Mary and Elizabeth can offer us an image of mutual, supportive friendship. They are two women who, in a time of great crisis and transition, supported each other, welcomed each other, understood each other. They reached out across age and difference to connect in loving embrace. They recognised within each other the embryonic new life which had not yet come to term, but was incipient within them. In a time of uncertainty and unknowing they were present to and for each other.

Images of the Visitation are passed around the group in silence. Time is taken to reflect on the images. Individuals could be invited to offer any comments.

Read the following, or some other suitable reading on friendship (e.g. the poem 'Friendship', by Elizabeth Jennings):

> Friends are those with whom we can be ourselves, let our hair down, weep, laugh, rage and lament without fear of rejection. We can try out new ideas on them, say what we really believe, dare to think aloud. Friends are those who accept us as we are, yet also recognise what we can be and, by their belief in us, help to bring new life to birth in us. The image of the two pregnant women meeting and celebrating the unborn life in each other can be a powerful symbol to us all, men and women, of this work of friendship which celebrates and supports new life into being in the other.
>
> Friends come in many different shapes and sizes. As in the case of Mary and Elizabeth, there may be a large age gap. Friendship can also extend across differences of race, culture, gender, class and lifestyle. Perhaps more than any other human bond, friendship is a free and inclusive love. We do not choose our families, we are born into them. We may choose our partners, yet often there is a sense of compulsion about falling in love that makes us feel we do not choose! Our friends are those we love simply because of who they are. And, unlike romantic or sexual partnerships, friendship can be a truly inclusive bond. In principle, there is no limit to the number of friends we can have, though in practice we may have limited energy and time to commit. Though friends can undergo conflict, misunderstanding and change, friendships which survive these challenges are cemented into strong and lasting bonds.[11]

A naming and celebrating of our friends

The leader introduces this naming of friends with the following, or other suitable words:

Leader: We give thanks for Mary's intimacy with Elizabeth:
            the intimacy of being recognised and known;
            the intimacy of being held and embraced;
            the intimacy of being encouraged and affirmed.

            We take time to give thanks for the intimacy we experience in friendship:

Individuals are invited to name the friends they wish to remember. People could be invited to bring Christmas cards as a symbol of their friendships and as a prompt to memory. This naming can go on for quite some time!

Closing affirmation

The following is said around the circle, with a different individual saying each stanza:

> I do not stand alone
> but with others to support me
> I will stand my ground.
>
> I do not see the way
> but with others to walk it with me
> I can make a path.
>
> I do not possess the truth
> but with others to witness to what they know
> I will be able to discern what is right.
>
> I cannot master all skills
> but with others who will lend their accomplishments
> I can do enough.
>
> I cannot carry every burden
> but with others to share it
> I may bear my own load.
>
> I cannot meet all needs
> but with others to nourish and replenish me
> I will be able to give enough.

I do not have limitless free choice
but with others to consult
I will make my own choices gladly.

I will not always be consistent
but with others to laugh at me
I will regain my equanimity.

I am not invincible
but with others to reach out a hand
I may learn from my mistakes and start again.

I cannot be perfect
but with others to make up the shortfall of my imperfections
I can be content to be good enough.

The liturgy may end with all standing in a circle holding hands in silence.

Nicola Slee

No room at the inn
Cropthorne liturgy 3

A Christmas Eve liturgy for people who feel disenfranchised by Christmas expectations and pressures.

Preparation

You will need candles in holders for the journey. Wrap up warm if you're going outside!

Background

'No room at the inn' is a liturgy about the sense of exclusion that all of us who attended the Cropthorne Christmas had felt in different ways at Christmas. As no one in the group subscribed to the married family norm so often portrayed by the media and advertising at this time of year, our sense of exclusion was in part about that. The liturgy symbolically enacts a journey to find a place of welcome and belonging. It began at 11.45 pm on Christmas Eve and deliberately started outside. After the census call, when it was clear that we did not match up to the requirements, we embarked on a symbolic journey around the garden of the house where we were staying, marking our exclusion from the domestic warmth of Christmas. We stopped at three 'stations'. One of these stations was by a single candle burning outside the chapel of Holland House. The group then approached the house, attempting to find a door where we could enter. We knocked first on the door of the chapel, only to find it locked, and then on another door symbolising the family; this too was locked. The third door we tried allowed us to step back on to the threshold of the community we had formed that week. We then moved into the warmth of the lounge – a room where we had shared laughter, tears, discussion, relaxation and other reflective liturgies. Here we danced a circle dance by candlelight to greet Christmas Day.

As this liturgy was written by two people we used two main speakers, but more could easily be used.

Opening call

A: Mary and Joseph could find no room
       when they came to Bethlehem
       because a census had been called by Caesar Augustus.

       Everyone was to be named and known officially,
       reporting and registering in their home town.
       Bethlehem was full to bursting
       on that night when they arrived
       with people eager to be legitimate
       (what penalty if they did not comply?).

       They could not find a place to stay
       because the demands of the loudest ruling voices in their society
       outstripped the human provision of warmth and comfort.

       There was no room at the inn,
       but they thanked God indeed
       for the innkeeper who allowed them to rest in his stable.

       On that night they could only find the light outside.

The census

A: A new census has been called tonight!
       How do we measure up?
       Have we all complied with the Christmas census?

B: Hear these cries of Advent!

A: Where is your family?
B: Where are your children?
A: Why have you all forgotten to get married?
B: Why don't you want to be with your family?
A: How much have you spent on presents?
B: Why haven't you sent a round robin letter detailing the banalities of last year
       and omitting anything meaningful?
A: How much have you eaten and drunk?
B: Why can't we hear your noise, see your waste, taste your enforced jollity?

A: There is no room at the inn of this Christmas for us.
        Let us therefore make our own journey
        through the darkness
        to find a door where we are welcome.
        We travel through the night.

ALL: SO WE CAN ONLY FIND THE LIGHT OUTSIDE.

The journey

B: We journey through a land
        where we are pitied
        because we have not been able to create the expected family.

ALL: SO WE CAN ONLY FIND THE LIGHT OUTSIDE.

B: We journey through a land
        where we often feel lonely in the family group
        and have to subscribe to the fantasy of the happy family,
        where we pretend all is well
        when really it feels out of tune.

ALL: SO WE CAN ONLY FIND THE LIGHT OUTSIDE.

Trying to find a way in

B: We knock on the door of the Church,
        but find there is no room for us
        amongst the unquestioned dogma,
        the triumphal trappings,
        the family services,
        and the patronising platitudes ...

ALL: SO WE CAN ONLY FIND THE LIGHT OUTSIDE.

A: We knock on the door of the family,
        but find there is no room for us
        amongst the comfortably heterosexual and married,
        amongst the competing needs of other people's desires for us at Christmas,
        amongst the nuclear family's insularity ...

ALL: SO WE CAN ONLY FIND THE LIGHT OUTSIDE.

The threshold

A: We knock on the door of the community
created this week at Cropthorne.
This door opens wide to greet us!

'In community life we discover our own deepest wound
and learn to accept it. So our rebirth can begin. It is from
this very wound that we are born.' (Jean Vanier)[12]

This strange child born today,
who has meant so much –
what is his coming to us now?
Did he come from a star of god?
Did he come from blood and earth?
Did he come as outsider,
to the outhouse?
Did he come out from under the heavy stone
of the Christmases we now bear?

ALL: WE COULD ONLY FIND THE LIGHT OUTSIDE,
BUT NOW WE STAND ON THE THRESHOLD
AND THE LIGHT HAS COME WITHIN US.

To the tune of 'O Come, All Ye Faithful':

O COME, ALL YE SEEKERS,
WEARY YET STILL HOPEFUL,
O COME YE, O COME YE,
TO BETHLEHEM;
COME AND EMBRACE HIM,
BORN THE FRIEND OF PILGRIMS:
O COME, LET US EMBRACE HIM,
O COME, LET US EMBRACE HIM,
O COME, LET US EMBRACE HIM,
OUTCAST AND FRIEND.

Inside

> *ALL:*   FOR THIS DAY, AND THIS CHRISTMAS WEEK,
> WE BELONG HERE:
> WE BELONG WITH EACH OTHER,
> AND WE BELONG TO EACH OTHER.
> WE HOLD EACH OTHER GENTLY
> AND THE LIGHT HAS COME WITHIN US
> AND ALL AROUND US.

Circle dance to greet Christmas Day

> *A:*   We welcome Christmas Day!
> The blessings of candlelight and starlight be upon us.
> The blessings of dream and sleep be upon us.
>
> Bright Morning Star,
> Gentle Lover of the Dance,
> Leap of Faith,
> Stillness of Joy,
> bless us this Christmas Day
> and all who journey with us.[13]

> *ALL:*   AMEN

Rosie Miles and Sue Tompkins

The muddle of the coming of God
Cropthorne liturgy 4

Introduction

In planning this liturgy we started with two images that we wanted to bring together: a difficult birth and the muddle of the coming of God.

We thought about the narrative of the birth of Jesus, and how it had been over-laid with so much imagery and had so much interpretation imposed upon it that it had become a sentimental fantasy, with the harshness and pain obscured.

We also talked about how many of our struggles with God-language are about a similar feeling of patterns being imposed and meanings being limited. We felt that much of this cheap religion comes from a desire to control experience and an anxiety to manufacture meaning, even where none has yet emerged.

We talked about our struggles to accept life as it is, rather than to control it. This is not to accept life with resignation, but to find a way to hold pain and confusion rather than rejecting and denying them: to integrate difficult experiences and accept the new life they can create. We tried to understand how this could be done. An image which seemed to help was that of Mary giving birth in pain and probably in fear, not at the time she would have chosen, not in the place she would have chosen, but nevertheless able to go with life and to give her energy to the act of creation.

We planned to create together a web, which would itself be muddled but which would hold our experience instead of excluding it. We planned to do this using balls of wool which we would toss back and forth to each other. In the worship, each person had their own ball of wool, but in order to create a web they had to give up control of it. Sometimes your ball would come back to you, but much of the time you had to watch it form a pattern within the group. Yet each person was still actively creating.

Creating the web

In advance of the liturgy we placed chairs in a circle, one for each person. A different-coloured ball of wool was tied to the right leg of each chair. We placed a card on each chair on which was written: 'For everything its season, and for every activity under heaven its time' (Ecclesiastes 3:1). Each card also had one of the following lines on it:

> a time to be born and a time to die;
> a time to plant and a time to uproot;
> a time to weep and a time to laugh;
> a time for mourning and a time for dancing;
> a time to seek and a time to lose;

a time to keep and a time to throw away;
a time to tear and a time to mend;
a time for silence and a time for speech.

To start creating the web, we joined in saying Ecclesiastes 3:1. Then one person read the line on their card and threw their ball of wool across the circle to someone. The person catching the ball wound it round the right leg of their chair a couple of times, then read their card and threw their ball of wool – and so on, until we had all thrown our wool. We then spent the next 20 minutes throwing the balls across the circle to one another, creating a tangled, multi-coloured web.

Once the web was complete we invited each other to place two objects in it (people had been told of this in advance) which represented (1) something you felt unresolved about and (2) something you felt a sense of resolution about. After this we had some time for quiet and contemplation, during which anyone was able to contribute their observations and feelings.

Following this, the last stanza of T.S. Eliot's 'The journey of the Magi' was read out.

Finally, we joined hands and said together:

FOR ALL THAT HAS BEEN – THANKS.
FOR ALL THAT IS TO COME – YES.
(Adapted from a poem by Dag Hammarskjöld)

Kate Lees, Ailsa McLaren and Anne Pounds

Liturgy of the gifts
Cropthorne liturgy 5

Introduction

In thinking about this liturgy three ideas were important to me. The first was that in the story of the Magi visiting Bethlehem the Magi all came from different places. This shows us that the work of the divine is found in all places, and perhaps particularly in unexpected places and people. There is also here the idea that something new is shown to those of us who move away from familiar ground in order to let our eyes be opened. Third, the idea of giving as receiving was significant. The Magi brought their gifts – they gave – but they received so much more from their visit to the Christchild. This belief that we nearly always give and receive at the same time became real to me when I visited El Salvador when it was in the middle of civil war. I visited a small village called El Burillo, which internal exiles had set up. The group who had been elected to run the village spoke with me through an American nun and told me about their fight to start the village. They showed me photographs of its beginnings: the planting of trees and the building of houses. I thought these photos were amazing and said so. Immediately the leaders said, 'Take any ones you want.' Would I have been able to offer my most prized possessions, just like that? I don't think so. I received far, far more than I gave.

Giving and receiving

We began by spending some time in the room that had been set up as a craft room at Holland House. I wanted everyone to leave Cropthorne with a sense of what they had to give, as well as with a sense of what, in their dreams, they needed or wanted to receive. On sheets of paper people were invited to write, draw or paint:

> Three things they had to give.
> Three things they needed.

We took about 20 minutes over this, in silence, with quiet music playing. At the end, people were given the option to share what they had written or to keep their thoughts private.

Finding gifts

We then travelled to another part of the house, where I had hidden everyone's present bags. This was to symbolise the importance of gifts in hidden parts of our lives and our need to travel to find them.

Prayer to the four corners of the Earth

Once we had all found our present bags, we gathered in a circle and said a prayer to the four corners of the Earth (see *Earth Prayers*, Harper San Francisco, pp.192–193; *Return Blessings*, Diann Neu, Wild Goose Publications, pp.100–102; or search on Google under 'Prayer of the four directions'). Or you could choose another prayer or poem or write your own. Choose a prayer or poem that is a reminder that Christmas is not about being insular and shutting out others. We are connected to people around the world in personal/political ways, and to the turning of the seasons and the Earth.

Receiving gifts

Finally, we opened our present bags and concluded with an Epiphany blessing:

> Go in peace.
> And may the God who protected the Holy Child
> cover you and keep you,
> the God who came to be with us
> be found beside you,
> and the love within you
> be called into safe places by the gentle Spirit.

Kate Fyfe

Here and now?

A meditation

Our minister, preaching in Advent, asked us where we saw ourselves in the nativity story. As a lesbian, I feel a sense of exclusion from the predominant, nuclear family imagery around the nativity; so I felt drawn to do meditations several years in a row to see where I fitted into the story. This is what came to me the first year:

I live in Bethlehem, a market town in Palestine. News has gone round of the arrival in town of a couple who have just had a baby – they are taking shelter in the barn belonging to Samuel since they can't find anywhere else to stay. There is some talk about strange goings-on related to this couple and their story. There's something about their arrival in town which won't let me rest. I have to see things for myself; so I decide that I'll go and find out if they need anything.

I throw on a shawl, slip out of the house, and follow the narrow way into town, tripping over ruts and rubbish in the dark. I find my way down to old Samuel's barn. Sure enough, a baby has been born. Its mother looks pretty exhausted. The father is older, kindly, yet looks worried about all the commotion. Some shepherds have arrived. Country people. They're saying that a whole sky-full of angels appeared to them while they were in the fields. The angels said to come here to worship this baby, because he is born of God and will fulfil God's purposes. Joseph is listening to their story, which they're telling over and over again in their astonishment. He's trying to get details out of them as to what exactly the angels had told them.

I look at the baby, all wrapped up and lying asleep in the hay. He looks like any other baby! Can it be that this child is to grow into someone who will be important in fulfilling God's plan for us? I find it hard to believe; but there's something going on, there's no doubt about that – something special and out of the ordinary. Things do happen! We're told to expect it. Why shouldn't it be here and now?

I talk to the mother. She assures me she has all she needs, that people are being kind. Her eyes look into mine with a sense of wonder through the exhaustion. I'm moved to say to her, 'Thanks be to God.' She smiles and nods.

I slip away. The shepherds are still talking with Joseph. Others like me have popped in to see what all the commotion is about. I walk away slowly, pondering. There's a feeling of expectancy and excitement in the dark night. Why shouldn't this be the moment? Here and now.

Francesca Rhys

Prayers on the theme of coming in from the cold

A bowl of sand with a tall, lit, gold and white candle (representing Christ) planted in it and a supply of small, unlit candles of different colours are set in the centre of the worship space.

A: We pray for people who are without shelter – for refugees, asylum-seekers, homeless people ... that they may come in from the cold ...
        To these people, we say:

ALL: YOU ARE THE DWELLING PLACE OF THE HOLY ONE.

B: We pray for people where the warmth of 'home' is absent due to incarceration; or insecurity; or professional, bureaucratic care ... We pray for children in care, elderly people in care homes, prisoners in jails, people in hostels, women and children escaping domestic violence and living in refuges ... May they come in from the cold.
        To these people, we say:

ALL: YOU ARE THE DWELLING PLACE OF THE HOLY ONE.

C: We pray for people who are excluded and discriminated against – lesbian, gay, bisexual and transgendered people, travellers, disabled people, minority ethnic groups, that they too may be welcomed in from the cold ...
        To these people, we say:

ALL: YOU ARE THE DWELLING PLACE OF THE HOLY ONE.

D: We pray for people known to us – for our families, our communities, our friends, those to whom we are close and those from whom we are separated; we bring them all in from the cold ...
        To these people, we say:

ALL: YOU ARE THE DWELLING PLACE OF THE HOLY ONE.

E: We pray for ourselves. We are brought into Christ. We come in from the cold and to ourselves, we say:

ALL: I AM THE DWELLING PLACE OF THE HOLY ONE.
        MAY I DO GOD'S WORK IN THE WORLD. AMEN.

People are invited to come forward to light one of the small candles from the Christ candle, and to plant their candle in the sand beside it – as a prayer for people left out in the cold or as a symbol of solidarity.

Gaynor Harper

Cropthorne Christmas blessing

The blessings of
bubble bath and bacon,
divas and desire,
fairies and feasting,
            be ours.

The blessings of
lIturgy and love,
walking and wanting,
cooking and creating,
            be ours.

The blessings of
friendship and fire,
weaving and wine,
Jenga and joy,
            be ours.

The blessings of
poetry and pleasure,
tears and touching base,
solitude and sleep,
            be ours.

The blessings of
talking and tasting,
presents and peace,
struggle and sexuality,
            be ours.

The blessings of
hugging and holding,
dancing and delight,
laughter and lunch,
            be ours.

The blessings of
candles and craft,
women and whisky,
leftovers and longing,
            be ours.

The blessings of
preparation and porcinis,
gay men and ginger, honey, orange and wine vinegar sauce,
hurting and healing,
                    be ours.

All these rich blessings,
the blessings of Cropthorne and Christmas,
be ours this night,
and all the days of our lives.

Rosie Miles

Chapter Twelve
Alternative Voices on Christmas

Last year, at the Lesbian and Gay Christian Movement carol service in Birmingham, we sang 'Once in Royal David's City'. We were seated in a circle. When we came to verse three, with its lines telling us that Jesus did nothing but 'honour and obey' throughout his 'wondrous childhood', and its final exhortation that 'Christian children all must be/Mild, obedient, good as he', laughter erupted from all sides. It wasn't the fact that some of the people there were gay and lesbian that made the lines funny per se – although perhaps we had less automatic deferential reverence towards the 'doctrines' set out in what we were singing than some – but more that the model of childhood we were being given seemed faintly ridiculous. Cecil Alexander, who wrote the words, was undoubtedly a man of his Victorian era. We may be lovers of traditional Christmas carols, but sometimes the saccharine nature of their sentiments just doesn't work in a contemporary age.

There are many voices not heard at this time of year because they don't chime in with the Christian-sanctioned sentimentalisation of such carols or the cultural will-to-merriment so prevalent. Some of the poems in this chapter are thus quite sober – reality checks amidst away-in-a-manger tweeness and the surface sparkle and glamour of tinsel. Not all pain can be wrapped up and hidden away. Other pieces offer a more humorous and wry sideways glance at the Christmas story and season. We are also reminded here that the 'little town' of one of our most beloved Christmas carols is a very real place, with its own tensions and brokenness.

Christmas shouldn't be …

Christmas shouldn't be like this:
hollow loneliness filled only with sorrow and bitter anger,
hope extinguished by cold sight and sound.
Bars and key chains replace pubs and jingle bells.

There's no homecoming this Christmas:
no gentle Jesus meek and mild,
no plastic doll nativity and angel children,
no silent, holy night muffling reality.

There's only this prison: harsh as stable stench,
lonely as death-threatened exile.
God's homecoming knew no comfort either:
unspoiled gift of life in our captivity.

Sally Buck

Holy town

What have they done to the 'Little Town'?
Imprisoned it in a concrete wall
Bethlehem – once a holy city
Trapped inside a ghetto wall.
Here where angels sang of peace
Where love and hope were born anew
Once surrounded by a heavenly host
Now surrounded by a concrete view.

Yet people crushed and hidden away
Still celebrate on Christmas Eve
Lighting candles for the child –
They still remember – still believe.
So light a candle this Holy Night
For Bethlehem and Beit Sahour
And for all the people caught inside
That cold and grey prison wall

Longing for a world of peace
Where all are treated equally

Where all can recognise their worth
Where all can live with dignity –
Where all can join hands with neighbours
Whether Muslim, Christian, Jew
And find a way to live together
Making Holy dreams come true.

Garth Hewitt

Broken town

Broken town of Bethlehem
Your people long for peace,
But curfews, raids and closure barricades
Have brought them to their knees
Still they strive for justice
Still they make their stand
Their hopes and fears still echo down the years
Come, heal this holy land.
Heal this holy land.

Holy child of Bethlehem,
Royal refugee,
Your place of birth is now a hell on earth
Through our complicity.
The innocents still suffer,
Their backs against the wall.
We see the curse, the violence and worse
And choose to ignore it all.
Choose to ignore it all.

Holy streets of Bethlehem
Deserted and destroyed
Frightened faces fill the sacred places
Pilgrims once enjoyed.
In the midst of darkness
A hopeful beacon shines:
The future lies in humble sacrifice
And not in guns and mines.
Not in guns and mines.

Holy star of Bethlehem
Help us to watch and pray.
With love and light illuminate the night
Reveal the Kingdom's day.
Dare us to be angels
Your awful truth to tell.
It must be heard:
You are the final word,
Our Lord, Emmanuel.
Our Lord, Emmanuel.

Martin John Nicholls

No walls

No walls.
                    But I am held captive.
No ceiling.
                    But I am pressed down.
No roof.
                    But I am covered over.
No doors.
                    But I am locked out.
No windows.
                    But I am still broken.
No floor.
                    But I share
                            your
                                earth.

Tony Walsh

matt and luke got hitched
december ceremony
make the yuletide gay

Rosie Miles

Feast

Not for me, claggy meat anaemic and dry,
cindered stuffing and parsnip à la mort.
Not for me sludged sprouts and peas,
oil slick spuds and last year's cranberry sauce.

This Christmas will be
Diwali Hanukkah Eid Christchild feast all in one:
with zalabia's oozing crunch my diet shall be undone,
rugelach rugelach let me bathe in your melt,
soufganiot tickle my lips with your doughnutty dough,
oh aloo gobi gulab jamun muttar paneer come,
be my delight, make my waistband tight,
hear my longing sigh ...

And if I must, for the sake of good form,
I might, as it's Christmas, eat a mince pie.

Rachel Mann

Genealogy

Matthew 1:1–17

He came from a dysfunctional family.
And I'm not just talking about his mum and dad
(the pregnancy out of wedlock,
the pronounced age difference)
No, it went back much further than that.
There were more than a few skeletons in his cupboard.

Take great King David,
the one they all wrote and sang about, eulogised in the histories,
the family's pride and joy.
He wasn't all he was cracked up to be, believe you me.
He might have been Jesse's golden-haired youngest,
but later, he was conniving and horny,
spying on his officer's comely wife from the palace balcony
and taking her for his own,
sending soldiers to do away with unsuspecting Uriah
returning victorious from battle. Some victory!

Prostitutes and foreigners aplenty scatter the litter:
women you'd not want your daughters taking after,
even if you can't help admiring that plucky Rahab.
Some came to a very sorry end.
That poor Tamar! It makes me shudder to even think of her.
Don't let your children read her story,
it'll keep them awake for nights on end.

Best not to ask about the ones
whose names have sunk into obscurity,
for fear of what you might uncover:
what unimaginable sleights of hand, sexual perversions,
brutal slayings or tortures.
Who now thinks of Nashon or Asa,
Uzziah, Joham or Jeconiah,
Matthan, Azar or Eliud?
Don't disturb their memories with your inquisitive fingers.

Keep going back and you end up at Abraham,
another one no better than he ought to be and a whole heap worse.
Right bastard, if you'll pardon my English.
Played off his wife as his sister, he did,
had it away with his slave girl to get himself a son
and then didn't lift a finger in her defence
when Sarah sent her packing into the desert
in a fit of jealousy and rage.
Worse of all, he was ready to kill his own precious Isaac
on some highfalutin whim of the Almighty.
That story has been causing trouble for generations
down the family line,
still keeps the menfolk and their offspring fighting.

No, not what you'd call a promising pedigree.
Not surprising he didn't turn out a happy family man.
Little wonder he stayed single.

Nicola Slee

The song of the angels (sometimes called the Gloria): A rap

Luke 2:8–20

Tune: any good strong rap beat – the funkier the better!

The swingin' shepherds:

Gotta stoke the fire.
Gotta get more heat.
Gotta rub our hands.
Gotta stamp our feet.
Gotta graft all night
Justa pay the bills.
Gotta stay awake.
Gotta pop no pills.
Gotta watch these sheep.
Gonna get no break.
Cos a shepherd's life
ain't no piece o' cake!

Chorus (twice):

Glory, glory, rap,
Make the heavens ring!
Glory, glory, rap,
Sing man, let it swing!

The rappin' angels:

Gotta rap the sky.
Gotta make it sing.
Gotta rise and shine.
Gotta shake a wing.
Gotta text these guys.
Gotta make 'em move.
Gotta shake 'em up.
Get 'em in the groove!
Gotta space 'em out.
Gotta make 'em go
down to Bethlehem
for the Glory Show.

Chorus (twice)

The swingin' shepherds:

Gotta GO MAN, GO.
Gotta make it BIG.
Gotta do this rap
at the Glory Gig.
Gotta go and see
just what's goin' down.
Gotta leave these sheep.
Gotta go to town.
Gotta find this kid.
Gonna take a fleece.
Gonna give RESPECT
to the Prince of Peace.

Chorus (twice)

Jean Mortimer

*Written for the children and young people of St Andrew's United Reformed Church,
Roundhay, Leeds, and performed by them with great gusto.*

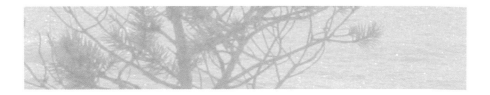

Away in a manger

In the manger next door there's a terrible din
when I'm meant to be getting my sleep,
but they're toasting an end to original sin
and plotting that Herod may weep.
For all their carousing, our stall here is quiet –
my coming prompts no social whirl;
my parents are freezing, our lamps shed scant light ...
and I think it's because I'm a girl.

Those shepherds and wise men who followed that moon
arrived here to find they'd a choice:
two families out in the unheated gloom,
two newborns both equal in voice.
They could have tossed coins, made some pretence,
let new history pages unfurl –
but they didn't think twice, didn't sit on the fence ...
and I know it's because I'm a girl.

It might have been different, you see, if they'd said,
'Hell, it's time for a woman to try.
We'll see what she makes of this business called life,
of the values that men might deny.
Let's loose her on wars and famines and drought,
on politics, passion and sport.
Will she rise to the challenge, make changes throughout?'
I'm a girl, so I guess that I ought.

But I might have said, 'No! Let's travel new roads,
and start in sustainable ways.
Can't we value diversity, share all the loads,
live hopeful and well-balanced days?
Let's not worship hierarchy, status and strength;
let's tear up the rule books right now.'
But those men didn't listen, strode straight past my bench ...
past the girl child who wouldn't know how.

Well, let them all party, their boy child on course –
I can't envy career paths like that;
I'm just sorry that two thousand years will endorse
the priorities this night begat.
But the future is female, perceptions will shift –
while we wait through one long, sidelined night
for those next doors to open, oppression to lift ...

I'm a girl. I suspect that I'm right.

Frances Green

This year I'm not coming

While visiting basic Christian communities in Italy, Ian M. Fraser collected the following poem-prayer. It was written by thirteen-year-old Massimiliano Tortis for Christmas Eve mass held in the public square. The mass was attended by almost the whole town, notwithstanding the freezing cold; no one went to the parish church mass. The following is a translation of the poem-prayer.

This year I'm not coming.

I'm not coming because I'm fed up with coming every year.
On your earth no one listens to me.
I speak of friendship and you kill each other.
I told you to help each other and instead you think of yourselves.
I told you to become poor and instead you always strive to become rich.
I told you to break bread with the hungry and you exploit them.
I told you not to rob and you instead make away with the money of the poor.

How can I come on your earth – which I gave you!

How can I come on an earth divided into two categories: 'haves' and 'have-nots'.

How can I come on an earth which calls itself civil and then kills its brother?
Listen to me closely. I have but one thing to say:

Repent, because the kingdom of heaven is near.
And you rich ones, pharisees and exploiters, will not enter my kingdom.
No!

It will be those whom you have treated as beggars,
as Cafoni*, as ignorant, who will enjoy eternal life.
I gave you the Word in order to place it at the disposition of the weak,
but you have made it private property to exploit the humble.
I told you to preach my words,
but you have closed yourselves in large buildings.

Many babies are born in your world just as I was in a stall:
a bare and dark stall
in which mothers fear that the baby will awake because they have nothing to give it;
but you don't even look at them.

You beat people because of the colour of their skin.
On Christmas, instead of thinking about the poor,
you enjoy yourselves eating and drinking.
You treat the poor like you treated me.
But I say to you:

Blessed are those who cry, for they will be consoled.
Blessed are those who are hungry, for they will be satisfied.
Blessed are those who are naked, for they will be clothed.
My kingdom will be composed precisely of these.

* Could be translated as 'human trash'

little town of
dreamless sleep, dark streets, fears,
all the years

Rosie Miles

Baby Jesus

'In your prayers,' the preacher says,
'approach the crib and see your saviour.
What gifts do you bring to him today?'

A cervix burnt and cauterised;
ovaries bearing host to cysts;
a barren body repulsed
by a child that abhors this womb.

'What would you like to say to Jesus?'

Nothing. The hurt must not be voiced.
His infancy is painful, but soon he will be grown.
Then we can talk.

But for now –
     for all the women in whom this child births naked pain,
     for all the men in whom this child arouses infertile longing,
     for all of us in whom this child creates a sense of incompletion –

'Mother Mary, hold our prayers.'

Karen Jobson

baby left by the bins
birmingham women's hospital
freezing fog tonight

Rosie Miles

Is this not Joseph's son?

In the shadows, silent, scarcely mentioned,
omitted from the first family pictures,
where are you,
who are you,
why have we lost you?

Old Doris Moon in Notting Hill
gave me a print of Georges de La Tour's
Christ with St Joseph in the Carpenter's Shop:
no halos, no angels,
just your form, glimpsed in the darkness.
Your face and his face
lit through flickering light,
a candle in his hand.

Were you as the painting shows,
thick in body frame,
arms like tree trunks,
hands strong yet gentle?
Your face bearded, weather-beaten,
radiant, grief-stained –
a well-lived-in face,
forged through interiority.

Handler of wood, worker with nails,
trusted tradesman, master craftsman of Nazareth.
Mary's man, house-builder,
home-maker, love-maker,
rough, tender, intimate man.

And what of your fathering
throughout those hidden years:
the hand-holding,
the addressing of soul,
the standing in his tracks?

What of your fathering through the awakening:
his rising and falling and rising yet again,
his playfulness,
his stretching out,
his reaching deep,

the knowing and the unknowing,
the painful acquisition of life wisdom,
the fearful learning of where faithfulness could lead?
Did you teach him to grow into calling God 'Abba'?
Did he learn from you the prayer, 'Father, into your hands I commend my spirit?'

Whom do you see when you look into the face of your child?
What of the son who has grown beyond you?

Well-earthed Joseph,
can you help us with our rough animality?
Can you father us into being,
a birthing within our complex fragility,
born again into our own resilient humanity?

Dear old Doris Moon,
who never knew her father,
thank you for the gift of Joseph –
father Joseph.

Donald Eadie

*'Christ with St Joseph in the Carpenter's Shop' was painted circa 1635–40 and hangs
in the Musée du Louvre, Paris.*

Mary and Joseph

And they are coming
not footsore, cursing a lazy donkey
but hidden, stifled and breathless
in the jackhammer hold of a container truck.

And their memories writhing
the memories of fists and shouting and running
and the eyes of soldiers, the veins of their eyes
the crack of rifle butt on bone and the screaming
memories writhing like eels in a bucket.

And they are coming
clasping each other, soothing and rocking
and chattering prayers
hot as fingers forced into fire.

And the child within kicking and bloating
scratching her insides and wanting out
and her wanting it out and wanting out
of the pitch and roll of the steel belly
her soft insides aching for the promised land to come.

Rachel Mann

Without right of abode

Her Majesty's Prison, Haslar, Gosport, UK

Refugees from tyranny
plead for asylum.
Prison closes around them
while they wait.
Language is a useless tool:
no one understands.

Outside the wire
encircling winds worsen.
Gales rock the hillside,
seas advance. Around the world
top statesmen double-talk,
confuse and threaten.

Christmas gains admission
without visa or tinsel.
The dispossessed share common ground.
Ancient chants and modern prayers
harmonise in a Babel-mix of tongues.

Hope lights the chapel for an hour,
passed hand to hand.

Edna Eglinton

not one room here. stop.
getting rather desperate –
mary soon to pop.

(joseph sends a telegraph home)

Rosie Miles

Chapter Thirteen
Midwinter Darkness

In the northern hemisphere, the fact that Christmas comes amidst darkest, coldest winter and broadly coincides with the winter solstice and the turning of the year offers rich metaphorical pickings. The year's calendar is actually encouraging us to hunker down, huddle together and hibernate amidst the extroverted glitz of the shopping high street. Turning towards the dark – with its mystery, silences and unknowns – is an inward journey that several pieces in this chapter encourage us to make. At the same time we also sometimes need light and warmth to help us through the long nights. Who knows what gift may be given when the darkness is at its deepest?

Advent calendar

1   Learn again the season's lessons:
2   Darkness. Tiredness. Tears.
3   Tenderness and memory.
4   Adult, driven by compulsive needs, let go.
5   Learn failure, self-acceptance.
6   Welcome laughter where it mingles with all things troubled and trembling.
7   Decide to do it differently.
8   Practise simplicity.
9   Make your choices with single-minded sincerity.
10 Rip up the round robin.
11 Declare a fast on enforced jollity.
12 Choose justice in place of sadness.
13 Clothe yourself in loving kindness.
14 Welcome the stranger – in yourself as well as in your neighbour.
15 Look for a neighbour where you're not expecting.
16 Unwrap Christmas presents in the greetings of strangers:
        shoppers jostling you on the high street.
17 Let the TV news rouse you to tears.
18 Let tears take you to action for goodness.
19 Turn down the tinsel.
20 Put on silence.
21 Let the season drive you to chasteness.
22 Let darkness sow seeds of contemplation
        where they may blossom: a single flower of compassion.
23 Cynic in you, become a child again.
24 Teach yourself starry-eyed wonder.
25 Become pregnant with hope and longing.
26 Child in you, looking for the perfect gift, learn disappointment.
27 Find treasure the other side of discarded wrappers.

28 Walk the days and nights of December you've forgotten
        and now remember.
29 Welcome winter's joys, its unspeakable sadnesses,
        God in straitened circumstances.
30 Bear the heart's chill, sudden lurchings and unsettlings.
31 Let your prayer be for the ones who live in that place always.

Nicola Slee

Cloister in the heart

berry on the green
silver on the sedge
scarlet on the leaf
  cloister in the heart

iron in the sky
freezing in the blood
purple on the sea
  cloister in the heart

wind across the land
rain upon the fields
birds along the sand
  cloister in the heart

death upon the wind
crying in the air
blood along the tide
  cloister in the heart

ripples on the mere
patterns in the sand
circles in the grain
  cloister in the heart

candles in the hearth
silence in the flames
ashes in the dark
  cloister in the heart

starlight on the roofs
shadows on the walls
peace upon the town
  cloister in the heart

Nicola Slee

A dream of Christmas

I'm dreaming of a quiet Christmas, a new Christmas, the first Christmas …

I'm dreaming of Advent as a time of waiting and not a time of rushing. Four peaceful weeks of anticipation where we prepare our souls rather than meals or presents. We could meet over a cup of tea and sit silently together, if you like. Did you know that I am happy when you are there, and happy when you are not there? Your presence and your absence are wonderful gifts.

At the right time, we brave the wilds of the garden centre and come home with a rich green tree. We drink wine as we garland the tree with lights and fetch out our ancient baubles and some new ones. We avoid the shops. We don't watch television.

It gets quieter and quieter. We expect no one; no one expects us. We find out who would like to be together on the quietest day of all, but are happy if it is just us.

On Christmas Day, we rise early, in silence, and we hardly say a word all day, for there is no time for speaking when there is so much looking to be done! Looks of love, looks of tenderness, looks of understanding, given and exchanged all day long. We hardly dare to go out lest we disturb the peace.

Time disappears and we float in a timeless place of peace and joy.

If we can be quiet enough, attentive enough, we may notice the Christ being born in us.

Kathleen Fedouloff

Out of the womb of darkness
A table liturgy for Advent

Every week at the Ark-T Centre, a community arts centre based in a church in Oxford, we share Communion at a table liturgy. We break bread, eat lunch and then continue to pray together afterwards. This is our liturgy for Advent.

(Note: Each person round the table reads a line until the Communion section when the liturgy is leader-led.)

Call to worship

> Full-bellied God, radiant mother of earth, luminous current in all of us,
> WE WAIT FOR YOU.

> Giver of the Christ, who took the fire of love into the heart of darkness,
> WE WAIT FOR YOU.

> Reckless Spirit, who flouts the darkness of prescribed ways and prejudice in her spangled dress,
> DANCE WITH US AND WITHIN US AS WE CELEBRATE YOUR LIFE AMONG US.

Confession of brokenness

> We come with the darkness in ourselves:
> the shadows of memory, troubled dreams and fears in the dark.

(We pause to reflect on our own brokenness and shortcomings.)

> We come with the darkness of our world:
> the unbroken cycle of damage to children, the failure of war, those whose past overshadows them, those for whom justice is not near.

(We pause to reflect on the events our world has seen this year.)

> We come with the unknown darkness that lies behind the lit windows in the streets around us and behind the faces of late night shoppers hurrying on their way.

(We pause to offer sorrow to God.)

> God did not wait till our lives were spotless.
> God did not wait till every child was loved.
> God did not wait till the hungry were fed.

God did not wait till the broken-hearted were comforted.
God came to a world such as ours to lighten the way, bring hope
and guide us into the ways of peace.

Reading (based on Genesis 1:1–4/John 1:1–5):

A: In the beginning when God created the heavens and earth ...

B: In the beginning was the Word, and the Word was with God, and the Word
         was God.

A: The earth was a formless void and darkness covered the face of the deep,
         while a wind from God swept over the face of the waters.

B: All things came into being through God, and without God not one thing
         came into being.

A: Then God said, 'Let there be light', and there was light.

B: What has come into being in God was life, and the life was the light of all
         people.

A: And God saw that the light was good; and God separated the light from the
         darkness.

B: The light shines in the darkness, and the darkness did not overcome it.

A time of sharing stories of darkness and light (stories from newspapers, personal stories, etc.)

Litany: Out of the womb of darkness

Out of the womb of darkness:
THE SPIRIT HOVERED OVER CREATION AS HER WATERS BROKE,
AND EARTH AND ALL THAT EXISTS CAME INTO BEING.

Out of the womb of our world's darkness:
WE SEEK THE HOLY PATH THAT REFUSES
THE EXCLUSION OF ONE GROUP BY ANOTHER.

Out of the womb of this community's darkness:
WE DARE TO BIRTH THE LIGHT OF CREATIVITY AND WELCOME.

Out of the womb of the winter darkness:
WE JOURNEY DEEP INSIDE WITH SACRED INTENTION
AS NIGHTS DRAW IN TOWARDS THE SHORTEST DAY.

Out of the womb of our own darkness:
WE REVEAL BEFORE THE LOVING GAZE OF GOD
OUR FEARS AND BROKENNESS, OUR HIDDEN HOPES AND LONGINGS.

Out of the womb of Advent darkness:
WE WAIT IN HOPE FOR A GOD WHO COMES AS KIN,
HOLDING OUT A NEWBORN'S TINY HAND.

Eucharistic prayer

Leader: God, come down from your place; be born in our world and lighten our hearts this Advent. Cross the threshold from heaven to Earth here in this meal. Pour out your Spirit on these bodily things that they may become for us the God whom we can see and touch and taste and hear and smell. For we long to sense you anew. We recall that time when ordinary people like us had supper with you. At your last meal with your friends, you took bread and broke it as a sign of what would happen to your body. You said: 'Take and eat. This is my body. Do this as often as you eat it in remembrance of me.' You shared a cup of wine, as a sign of your blood which would be shed when the midday sun went black, saying: 'Drink this everybody, for this is my blood shed as a sign of the new relationship between God and the Earth and all its peoples.'

Come, light of the world. Nourish us with your presence.
DRAW US TO YOURSELF, TO EACH OTHER,
AND TO ALL YOUR PEOPLE IN HEAVEN AND ON EARTH.

We pass round the bread and wine and then eat a lunch of bread, soup and cheese together.

Bringing others to the table

Leader: Let us name, in the silence of our hearts or aloud,
those people and situations where the longed-for hope needs to be revealed.

A candle is lit for each name said.

WE HOLD THESE PEOPLE IN OUR HEARTS AND
WAIT WITH THEM.

Closing prayer

May God wait with us
as we wait for the light of justice, peace and right relations,
with each other, with the earth and with our God.

We leave this place cherishing the darkness
THAT WE MIGHT KNOW THE LIGHT.
Blessed be the light-giver, the star-maker, the love-bringer.
THANKS BE TO GOD.

Tess Ward

Winter warmth

A knife, sharp and deadly, flashing as it reflects the light from a single bulb. I bring it carefully down upon the skin. It slices cleanly, a thin piece of flesh landing, like a tart fillet steak, upon the old wood of the table.

I repeat the cut another nine times until the lemon has been divided into ten even pieces, then do the same again to the second lemon and the two oranges, adding them to a gallon of red wine (made from the blackberries that overtook the orchard last summer) already warming under a low heat.

A handful of seeds from the *Myristica fragrans*, or nutmeg, is held in the hand for a moment, the aroma inhaled as I imagine the warm sirocco of its homeland in the West Indies and add the wish for warmth to the brew.

Cloves, those sweetly pungent flower buds of the *Eugenia caryophyllus*, are added next, their antiseptic properties added as a prayer for the good health of all those who drink my brew. The Chinese wrote of these tiny medicines as early as 400 BC, and used them to treat nausea, dyspepsia and, naturally, bad breath.

The sweet bark of the *Cinnamomum zeylanicum* was used by the ancient Egyptians as medicine and in embalming. I inhale the sweet scent of the rolled bark, once considered more precious than gold, and add the desire for long life for my friends and family

As the potion begins to steam, I stir it three times widdershins, for the three faces of the Goddess, and add Demerara sugar, invoking the sweet warmth of Mauritius and the yellow sulphur of the earth. Finally, I add a jar of honey, for productivity and sweetness.

I centre myself and invoke the Goddess, breathing her breath across the surface of the brew. By Air, Fire, Earth, Water and Spirit, I use the tip of the wooden spoon to etch a pentagram on the liquid surface, calling for the protection of all those who partake of this heady brew.

I lift the cauldron off the flames and carry it round the circle. Each man and woman takes a chalice, filled with all the strength I can offer, and we toast the Goddess and the Holly King on the Winter Solstice.

> Winter Solstice, winter's turn;
> Stack the fire with wood to burn;
> Goddess and God, we drink to Thee;
> Blessèd all, so mote it be!

Rachel Green

All-age elemental rites for December

Preparation

Set up a table with a cloth on it and a globe in the middle.

For each week in December choose an element (earth, air, fire, water) and place things relating to it on one quarter of the table (items can be placed daily or weekly). Below are poems, suggestions for items, prayers and weekly rituals.

A daily prayer, said whilst spinning the globe:

> Maker of the Universe
> light and dark
> turning us
> sustaining us
> in you we love
> in you we live
> and we are holy.

> **Weekly themes**

EARTH

> rooted
> nurtured
> tickled by centipedes
> sundered by stones
> on you we stand
> and you are holy.

Table items: plants, stones, fruit, leaves, toy tractor

Prayers: gardeners, town planners, park keepers, JCB drivers, those who work to keep the earth beautiful, those who live in dangerous environments

Weekly ritual: Plant some bulbs. Walk in the woods.

AIR

> blown
> tumbled
> sounded by bats
> soared by eagles

you we breathe
and you are holy

Table items: whistle, balloon, feather, flag, bubble mixture

Prayers: astronauts, steeplejacks, aeroplane crews, beekeepers, those who work to reduce pollution, those who live in polluted environments

Weekly ritual: Fly a kite. Blow bubbles in the open air. Have a turn on a swing.

FIRE

danced
blazed
breathed by dragons
exploded by stars
by you we are warmed
and you are holy

Table items: candles, coal, silver stars

Prayers: candle makers, chefs, firefighters, metal workers, those without warmth and shelter

Weekly ritual: Light a fire and dance around it. Have a winter barbecue. Light candles for those you love and cherish.

WATER

plodged
swallowed
wallowed in by whales
splashed about by children
you we drink
and you are holy

Table items: bowl of water, shell, pebble, seaweed, bottle of juice

Prayers: plumbers, lighthouse keepers, sailors, sewerage workers, those who work to keep seas and waterways free from pollution, those who have no access to clean water

Weekly ritual: Wash hands and feet in a bowl of warm water. Paddle in a local water source. Drink a local beverage.

Ruth Burgess

Colourful rites for December

Preparation

Choose a strong colour for each week in December: e.g. red, blue, yellow, green, black, silver, orange, white, purple. Set up a table with space and each week add items of your chosen colour.

E.g. Week 1 – Red – berries, leaves, toy bus, book cover, postcard, apples, etc.

Use natural items: flowers, leaves, fruit and vegetables, stones, wool.

Use manufactured items: pottery, ribbons, glass, metal, advertising material, toys, hankies

Choose a good time for you and use the items on the table as a focus for your prayers.

Have a family competition to see who can find items each day. You might need some boundaries: the object needs to fit on the table – and nothing that breathes and moves!

Have a meal each week with table decorations, food and participants' clothing relating to the appropriate colour.

Read or tell stories that bring in the week's colour.

Paint pictures each week using the week's colour.

Find songs to sing that include the week's colour.

Make Christmas presents using your chosen colours: a painting, a knitted scarf, an iced cake, bunches of dried flowers …

Give Christmas presents relating to all colours: kaleidoscopes, spinning tops, rainbow clothing, paints and crayons, crystals, different kinds of preserves and jams.

Ruth Burgess

Midwinter prayer

God of all creation
    of bare forest and low northern skies
    of paths unknown and never to be taken
      of bramble, sparrow and damp, dark e

we thank you for loss, for the breaking of the dimming year
we thank you for light, even in its seeming midwinter failing
we thank you for life, for its hope and resistance
like a seed dying and living.

Rachel Mann

It is winter

It is winter   cracking under ice
It is snow   sashaying between air to earth
It is sky   blue light through leafless trees
It is oak   raised bare fingers, veins and arms
It is sun   low burning candle white

It is a gap   a space   a breaking
It is a giggle a gurgle   a cry

Rachel Mann

fox and his gift

A friend who was a member of the Russian Orthodox Church gave me a beautiful carving of a fox in wood. It lies among other things by the candle on the table in my study. She also told this story.

It was darkest night and the night visitors had gone their way, leaving their gifts – the gifts of kings and of shepherds. The baby was asleep and the parents were resting after the long day. There were animals in the stable and all was quiet save for the sound of the swishing of the tail of the horse, the slow chewing of the cow and the hens pecking.

Suddenly there was a movement in the shadows. It was the fox.

'What's an animal like you doing in a place like this?' asked the horse.

'I've come to bring my gift for the child,' the fox replied.

The other animals had woken and looked with amazement at the fox.

'What can an animal such as you bring to a child such as this?' said the cow.

The fox was silent. Then he spoke: 'This child, when he is fully grown, will need to know when to lie low in the dark shadows and when to move out into the light, wide, open spaces. This is the gift I bring.'

The animals looked at each other and laughed at the thought of such a thing. But when they stopped laughing and turned to look again into the dark shadows of the stable they realised that the fox had disappeared once more into the night, having left his gift for the child.

Donald Eadie

Seeing differently

This year has contained many experiences of seeing, as if for the first time. I am now on exercise number 50 of the 70 that make up my photography course. The experience of being taken out of my habitual way of looking led me from simply regarding a scene as I found it, to thinking about where I could put myself in it to see things differently.

Most recently I have been watching the light changing through the day. Moments of special lighting effects are often very fleeting as the sun interacts with the contours of a building, field or tree. Over months the changes are huge. I knew, of course, that the sun moved through the year but it has taken me 48 years to appreciate just how far the position changes, for example, from a summer sunset to a winter one. There are so many moments in time as light, colour, vegetation and wildlife change throughout the year. I wonder if I am experiencing the same excitement that the ancients felt as they watched for the solstice sunlight on their stones.

Waiting for the moment. Waiting an hour or a week or a month. Waiting with endurance, as wildlife photographers do, always hoping to be ready at the moment the longed-for one comes. (Those with the largest budgets can get technology to wait instead, but is that the same photographic event?)

All this leaves me wondering how I would photograph Christmas. What a huge theme. No one image could possibly begin to capture it all. Perhaps my prayer is that we would all expand inwardly, rather than outwardly, taking something to our hearts and minds as if for the first time.

Bridget Woollard

Pacemaker

Learn to sit still,
watch fire glowing.
Instead of dashing
seeing, knowing.

Shut the noise out,
hear wind blowing.
Instead of rushing
breathing, flowing.

Stand in one place,
feel pace slowing.
Instead of racing
being, growing.

Andrée Heaton

Heartbeat

From the clutter of sound and sense be still
from noise deep within and noise far without
from mind jam-packed with need and desire
just listen, listen to your heartbeat

For the time is rich and the time is full
and the time of your life is gently given
the time is now and the time is silence
to listen, listen to your heartbeat

All the striving, all the aching
all the longing unfulfilled
all the wanting, all the making
all the future willed

put it down, give it up
lay it out, throw it wide

and listen, listen to your heartbeat
    listen, listen to your heartbeat
    listen, listen to your heartbeat

Rosie Miles

A time to
Delve deeper into
the lo**V**e of God –
Emmanuel –
Not spending
Too much money.

Kitty Price

Sing high, sing low, swing free, let go

Tune: Noel

Sing high, sing low, swing free, let go,
God of the turning round,
In times of change may we discern
The true angelic sound.
For there are songs of gentler power
That warfare needs to hear;
These nurturing sounds will bring us strength
And make the peace song clear.

Sing high, sing low, swing free, let go,
God of the circling sphere,
In looking back may we discern
The times you have been near.
We face the joy, we touch the pain
And give you thanks for both;
We weave the two as glistening strands
Within our travelling coat.

Sing high, sing low, swing free, let go,
God of the open road,
In moving on may we discern
The contents of our load.
Help us to sift, help us to lose
All we no longer need,
That we may leap and dance and sing
At your God-chosen speed.

June Boyce-Tillman

The unchristmas tree

The unchristmas tree has no lights
except what filters through its spaces

no tinsel
except its own astringent needles

no star
except those caught in its branches

no presents
except the gifting of itself

The unchristmas tree costs nothing at all
except the grace to notice where it grows

Rosie Miles and Nicola Slee

Notes:

1. Polly Toynbee, from the New Humanist website **www.newhumanist.org.uk**

2. Haddon Willmer from 'Taking responsibility: The Future of Christianity in Our Hands', Haddon Willmer, from *20/20 Visions: The Futures of Christianity in Britain* (London: SPCK, 1992), p.132.

3. This text is taken from the 'Christmas Eve Service of Las Posadas', *United Methodist Book of Worship* (Nashville, TN: United Methodist Publishing House, 1992), p.282.

4. For scholarly studies of Christmas see M. Connelly, *Christmas: A Social History* (London: I.B. Tauris, 1999) and A. Kuper, *Unwrapping Christmas* (Oxford: Clarendon, 1993), pp.157–75.

5. For details of these studies see Eleanor Nesbitt's publications listed in *Intercultural Education: Ethnographic and Religious Approaches* (Brighton: Sussex Academic Press, 2004), and on **www.warwick.ac.uk/go/wreru/aboutus/staff/en/enpublications.doc**

6. Martin Stringer, *On the Perception of Worship: The Ethnography of Worship in Four Christian Congregations in Manchester* (Birmingham: University of Birmingham Press, 1999) p.196.

7. For further reading see Yasmin Alibhai, 'A White Christmas', *New Society 18* (December, 1987), pp.15–17.

8. Meera Syal, 'And I bet you have curried turkey as well ...', *The Guardian*, 27 December 1997.

9. Jane Still can provide details of the liturgy used for 'The journey of the Magi'. **still.family@virgin.net**. See also Joanna Bogle's *A Book of Feasts and Seasons* (Gracewing, 1992) and Paul F. Bosch and André Lavergne's 'Chalking the door' liturgy **www.worship.ca/docs/l_chalk.html**

10. Jane Still can provide details of the wassail liturgy she uses. **still.family@virgin.net**

11. 'Friends are those with whom we can be ourselves ...', by Nicola Slee, from *Remembering Mary* (Birmingham: National Christian Education Council, 2000), pp.52–3.

12. Jean Vanier, from *Community and Growth* (London: Darton, Longman and Todd, 1979), p.6.

13. This blessing in part uses words by Jim Cotter in *Prayer at Day's Dawning* (Sheffield: Cairns Publications, 1998), pp.20 and 126. Used with permission.

Sources and acknowledgements

Every effort has been made to trace copyright holders of all the items reproduced in this book. We would be glad to hear from anyone whom we have been unable to contact so that any omissions can be rectified in future editions.

'There is a beautiful spiritual message underlying Christmas that has universal appeal ...' by Rabbi Michael Lerner, from the Network of Spiritual Progressives website. Used by permission. www.spiritualprogressives.org

'Silence in the suburbs' – by Jean Mortimer, originally published in *Courage to Love: An anthology of inclusive worship material*, edited by Geoff Duncan, Darton, Longman and Todd, 2002, p.86. Used by permission of Jean Mortimer.

'December 24th' – by Sue Vickerman, first published in *The Social Decline of the Oystercatcher* by Sue Vickerman, Biscuit Publishing, 2005. Reproduced by kind permission of the publishers.

'Nativity: a short story' – by Mandy Ross, first published in *For Generations: Jewish motherhood*, edited by Mandy Ross and Ronne Randall, Five Leaves Publications in association with European Jewish Publication Society, 2005. Reproduced by permission of the publishers.

'UK Christmases in sociological perspective' – by Eleanor Nesbitt. The material forming the basis of this piece was originally published in Eleanor Nesbitt, *Intercultural Education: Ethnographic and Religious Approaches* (Brighton: Sussex Academic Press, 2004), and is reproduced here by permission of the publishers.

'Alternatives to buying' – from Pax Christi's leaflet *How Shall We Celebrate Christmas?*. Copies available from Pax Christi, Christian Peace Education Centre, St. Joseph's, Watford Way, Hendon, London, NW4 4TY. E-mail: paxchristi@gn.apc.org Used by permission of Pax Christi.

'I do not stand alone ...' – 'With Others: A Statement of Interdependence', by Nicola Slee, in *Praying Like a Woman* (London: SPCK, 2004), p.66. Used with permission.

'Holy town' – by Garth Hewitt © Chain of Love music. Administered by Daybreak Music Ltd., PO Box 2848, Eastbourne, BN20 7XP. Used by permission.

'Broken town' – by Martin John Nicholls, From the album *Beyond Belief* by Martin John Nicholls, © Daybreak Music Ltd. PO BOX 2848, Eastbourne, BN20 7XP. All rights reserved. info@daybreakmusic.co.uk International copyright secured. Used by permission.

'This year I'm not coming' – from *Reinventing Church: Insights from small Christian communities and reflections on a journey among them*, Ian M. Fraser. Used by permission of Ian M Fraser.

No walls' by Tony Walsh – first published in *Citizen 32* magazine, issue 2.

'Sing high, sing low, swing free, let go' – by June Boyce-Tillman © 2006 Stainer & Bell Ltd. P.O. Box 110, Victoria House, 23 Gruneisen Road, London N3 1DZ www.stainer.co.uk Used by permission.

About the authors

Agnes is a Christian, a mum to four and a nurse ... She fits in a few little extras, such as her befriending role, because God has given her far more blessings than she can possibly use herself.

Melanie Ashford is a strict vegetarian and is strongly against animal testing. She is 16, and her favourite subject in school was chemistry.

Gillian Ashley works in arts administration, and is also a part-time (slightly mature) university student, reading English literature. She is widowed, but friends, work, university and a greyhound named Bryn keep her busy and fulfilled.

Gail Ashton lives in Cheshire. She has published widely in various poetry magazines and anthologies. Her first collection, *Ghost Songs*, will be published by Cinnamon Press in 2007.

Christina Beardsley, an Anglican priest, was co-founder and first chair of the Clare Project for people dealing with issues of gender in Brighton and Hove.

June Boyce-Tillman read music at St Hugh's College, Oxford and has written widely on music, spirituality, healing and gender. She is a composer of liturgical music, a performer of one-woman shows based on the women mystics, and a hymn writer whose collection *A Rainbow to Heaven* will be published in 2006. She is Professor of Applied Music at the University of Winchester and Chair of the Alister Hardy Research Committee.

Ross Bradshaw is Nottinghamshire County Council's literature officer. He also runs a small press, Five Leaves Publications, which has just celebrated its tenth birthday www.fiveleaves.co.uk

Susan Britton is an activist who worked for Diakonia, the Durban-based church social action agency, for 24 years. She is a priest in the Anglican Church in South Africa.

Sally Buck works as an assistant chaplain in a women's prison, and is a Reader in the Church of England and a trained counsellor.

Helen Buckingham was born in London and now lives in Bristol. Her poetry has been published throughout the world. A sampler of her work, *Talking the Town Red*, can be obtained from Waterloo Press, Brighton.

Ruth Burgess lives in Sunderland with a large and hungry black and white cat. She works with people with dementia and is also a writer. She delights in fireworks and in home-grown rhubarb and raspberries.

Stephen Burns is Chaplain and Lecturer in Worship and Liturgy at St John's College,

Durham University. He is author of *Liturgy: SCM Studyguide* (SCM Press, 2006) and *Worship in Context: Liturgical Theology, Children and the City* (Epworth Press, 2006).

Jim Cotter writes and publishes as Cairns Publications and is currently engaged in a project to see how almost redundant churches can be brought alive as small pilgrim places. See www.cottercairns.co.uk and www.smallpilgrimplaces.org.uk

Chris Dowd is an ordained minister in the Metropolitan Community Church who began a different style of church in Birmingham in 2004. He lives with his partner, Will, and their two dogs, Bea and Honey.

'E' writes science fiction.

Donald Eadie is a father and a grandfather. He is also an adopted person. In recent years he has lived with a serious spinal condition and retired early as a Methodist minister.

Rowena Edlin-White is a freelance author of children's fiction and adult non-fiction, and has edited *Design Your Own Wedding Ceremony* (with Michael Perry), *Dancing on Mountains* (with Kathy Keay) (both HarperCollins) and a new collection of young adult fiction, *In the Frame* (Five Leaves). She is a Lay Reader in the Diocese of Southwell and Nottingham.

Edna Eglinton worked as a secretary in a variety of situations. Now retired, she enjoys writing poetry. She lives in Devon.

Kevin Ellis is a priest in the Anglican Diocese of Carlisle. He lives with his partner, Jennifer, two lurchers named Frodo and Pip, and a cat called Nelson. Jennifer and Kevin hope to adopt soon.

Ruth Farrer lives on a canal boat and is studying biblical studies at the University of Manchester. She has had articles published in women's magazines and hopes to write full-time after she graduates this summer.

Kathleen Fedouloff is a therapist living and working in Ireland. She is married and has two nearly grown-up children. She likes books, cats, music and the sea.

Kate Fyfe has worked in a variety of jobs, including nurse, health adviser in sexually transmitted diseases, and more recently in the International Relations Team at USPG (United Society for the Propagation of the Gospel). She was involved in experimental worship for 10 years in the Wimbledon Liturgy Group.

Frances Green is a London-based human resources manager grappling on a daily basis – like so many of us – with that tricky life/work balance. She loves creative writing, and has had several poems published over the last couple of years.

Rachel Green is a forty-something writer from the hills of Derbyshire. She lives with her two female partners, their two kids and their two dogs, and only occasionally gets them all mixed up.

Mary Grey is an ecofeminist liberation theologian and co-founder of Wells for India, a small NGO committed to water security and well-being for semi-desert villages in Rajasthan. Her most recent books are *Sacred Longings: Ecofeminist Theology and Globalisation* (SCM, 2003) and (with Dan Cohn-Sherbok) *Pursuing the Dream* (DLT, 2005).

Gaynor Harper is a teacher and writer who lives in a Gloucestershire village. For the past few years she has been organising retreats and quiet days for those on the margins of main-stream Christianity.

Sybil Harvey-Lago divorced many years ago. She regards Moseley, Birmingham as the centre of the universe and is grateful to Cadbury, her Chocolate Burmese, and Lisa, her Lilac Burmese, for allowing her to live with them.

Deborah Headspeath lives in Suffolk with her fiancé and a mad cat called Sybil. She has been working with asylum-seekers and refugees for the last five years.

Andrée Heaton worked throughout her career in education. Now retired, she is choosing to spend her time as creatively as possible. She enjoys writing poetry and pursuing a wide range of interests which professional commitments did not previously enable her to explore.

Garth Hewitt is a songwriter and author, and also an Anglican priest and social activist with a strong commitment to human rights. He is Director of the Amos Trust (**www.amostrust.org**), a peace and justice organisation. He has been writing and recording songs for over 30 years, and it has been his experiences of travelling around the world to many situations of poverty and conflict that have made him particularly committed to issues of justice and peace.

Jean Hickson is a member of the British Humanist Association and an accredited officiant for humanist ceremonies. She is also a soon-to-retire violin teacher.

Beryl Jeanne lived in Africa and now lives and worships in Birmingham. She is a tutor and retreat leader. Loves that sustain her include her family, open space, early mornings, people, playing with colour and words, and helping others to enjoy being creative.

Helen Jesty was one of the first women to be ordained in the Church of England. She works part-time at a local children's hospice and has been involved in Winchester Area Community Action for many years. She recently trained as a magistrate.

Karen Jobson works as a minister. She spent two years working as a teacher in Namibia.

Jo Jones worked for Christian Aid and her inspiration comes from the many people she met in the UK who are passionate to make the world a better place.

Peter Kettle is an Anglican priest in Greater London. He spent 10 years in full-time parochial ministry and (to date) has spent 15 years in secular employment, exploring life and ministry on the edge of the Church.

Anthony and Magnus Kramers are part of the ecumenical L'Arche Edinburgh community that welcomes people with learning disabilities, employed assistants and volunteers to a shared life founded on the values of simplicity, mutual faithfulness and accountability. Further community resources for shared prayer – songs, carols and texts – can be accessed via da_noust@yahoo.co.uk

Kate Lees' four-year-old god-daughter declared her to be her 'mother of God', which makes the rest of her biography seem rather uninteresting. Kate has found inspiration in liturgies drawn from life throughout many years in the Birmingham Womenfaith group.

Michael Lerner is a rabbi and co-chair of the Network of Spiritual Progressives with Cornel West and Benedictine Sister Joan Chittister **www.spiritualprogressives.org**. He is editor of *Tikkun* magazine and author of *The Left Hand of God: Taking Back our Country from the Religious Right* (HarperSanFrancisco, 2006). He lives in California.

Yann Lovelock is Vice Chair of West Midlands Faiths Forum and Interfaith Coordinator for the Network of Buddhist Organisations; he is also on the executive of Birmingham Council of Faiths and the West Midlands Buddhist Council.

Pam Lunn is a tutor at Woodbrooke, the Quaker adult college in Birmingham. She worked on a development project in Zimbabwe during 1985.

Jonathan Magonet has recently retired as Principal of Leo Baeck College, the London-based rabbinic seminary, where he teaches Hebrew Bible. He is the author of a number of books on the Bible, most recently *A Rabbi Reads the Bible* and *A Rabbi Reads the Psalms* (SCM).

Rachel Mann is an Anglican priest in Stretford, South Manchester. She has made contributions to a range of publications, including several Wild Goose anthologies. She is passionate about far too many things – poetry, wine, food, skiing, being lazy and theologies of sexuality and gender. Someday she plans to learn the piano.

Alwyn Marriage is a poet, author and lecturer currently working freelance as a writer and environmental consultant. She has been a university lecturer, director of two international aid agencies and editor of the journal *Christian*.

Tony McClelland is Senior Methodist Tutor at the Queen's Foundation for Ecumenical Theological Education, Birmingham.

Ailsa McLaren was raised as an Anglican, but her upbringing was actually dominated by Roman Catholic nuns, Quakers and Methodists. After a number of years working in higher education, she intended to keep goats on a Mediterranean island; instead she is studying nursing at Coventry University.

Rosie Miles has appeared in a number of Wild Goose anthologies and poetry magazines. She is remarkably fond of jelly and in her spare time teaches English at the University of Wolver-hampton.

Rachel Montagu is the Assistant Education Officer at the Council of Christians and Jews and teaches biblical Hebrew at Birkbeck College's Faculty of Continuing Education. She has worked as a congregational rabbi and is particularly interested in women's interfaith dialogue.

Jean Mortimer is a retired United Reformed Church minister, a former university lecturer in New Testament Studies, a freelance writer, a mother of two sons and a kite flier.

Jesse N.K. Mugambi is Professor of Philosophy and Religious Studies at the University of Nairobi, Kenya. He is an Anglican lay theologian with long experience in the ecumenical movement. His most recent book is *Christian Theology and Social Reconstruction* (Nairobi: Acton, 2003).

Judith Nathanail lives in Nottingham with husband, Paul, and sons, Peter and Alexander. She is a geologist who works part-time for an environmental consultancy. She worships at St Michael's, Bramcote.

Eleanor Nesbitt is Reader in Religions and Education at the Institute of Education, University of Warwick. Her publications include *Sikhism: A Very Short Introduction* (Oxford University Press, 2005) and *Intercultural Education: Ethnographic and Religious Approaches* (Sussex Academic Press, 2004).

Martin John Nicholls is a Christian singer/songwriter and aid worker based in the UK. He works for Christian Aid, informing and inspiring people to put their faith into action and to stand alongside the poor. He tours extensively with Campaign Cabarets and multimedia roadshows. **www.martinjohnnicholls.co.uk**

Pax Christi is an International Catholic Peace Movement open to all who are in sympathy with its gospel-based values and work. Pax Christi is involved in education and campaigning to create a world where people can live in peace, without fear of violence in all its forms. **www.paxchristi.org.uk**

Yvonne Peecock is an Essex girl and a third-generation atheist. Originally a drama student, she married a journalist and they had five children. Now grandma to 10, she is happily employed as a humanist celebrant and conducts weddings, namings and funerals.

Jo Perry was a volunteer teacher for a year in an international mission school in Tanzania.

Judith Phillips has been addicted to choral singing since childhood. She moved from a career in education to prison chaplaincy (in South West England) on a full-time basis six years ago. It's an immensely varied ministry – people who ask her 'What do you do?' get a blank look as she tries to think of where to start.

Pat Pinsent has taught for many years at what is now Roehampton University, where she is a Senior Research Fellow. Subjects covered in her books and articles include religious poetry, reading, children's literature and Christian feminism. She also edits *Network*, the journal of Women Word and Spirit.

Annie Porthouse is author of the chick-lit novels *Dear Bob* and *Love Jude* (published by Scripture Union). She is a freelance writer and blue cheese eater, who hangs out at www.annieporthouse.com

Anne Pounds was brought up in a strict Anglican liturgical tradition. In her middle years she joined with other women in composing liturgies for various situations, and was part of Women in Theology (WIT). In her later years she has become a Quaker. She lives in Grange-over-Sands, Cumbria.

Ianthe Pratt is coordinator of the Christian Women's Resource Centre in London, and co-author of a number of books on creative liturgy.

Kitty Price is intrigued by angels, adores chocolate, makes necklaces, writes haiku and lives in Portsmouth with her musical husband, David, and four crazy cats. She is training to be an RE teacher.

Jo Rathbone runs Eco-congregation, a programme to encourage churches to weave creation care into their life and mission www.ecocongregation.org. With husband, Dan, and children, Anna and Esther, she tries to build an ethical lifestyle at home.

Francesca Rhys was raised in London but has lived on four continents as a language learner and teacher. She is now fulfilling a life ambition by studying theology (for Methodist ministry) at the Queen's Foundation in Birmingham.

Robert Ritchie has worked as a civil servant for many years and is also a non-stipendiary priest in the Church of England. He is married to Sarah and they have a son, Theodore.

Susan Roll presently teaches at Saint Paul University, Ottawa, Canada, where she serves as Professor of Liturgy and Sacraments in the Faculty of Theology and Director of the Centre for Women and Christian Traditions. She has published in the areas of feminist liturgy, the liturgical year and pastoral theology.

Mandy Ross lives in Birmingham, where she belongs to the Progressive Synagogue. She combines writing children's books and teaching, and has a seven-year-old son, who was not born on 25th December.

Floe Shakespeare is a single, feminist lesbian and a Quaker who believes that all days are sacred.

Nicola Slee is a theologian and poet based at the Queen's Foundation for Ecumenical Theological Education, Birmingham. Author of *Faith and Feminism* (DLT, 2003) and *Praying Like a Woman* (SPCK, 2004), her second collection of poems and liturgical texts will be published by SPCK in 2007. She lives with Tinker and Pumpkin, two dotty cats, and Rosie Miles.

Jane Still finds it difficult to live 'in the moment' with her three children and vicar husband, but does her best!

Christine Terry lives in Birmingham and works as a nurse at the Queen Elizabeth Hospital. She is a Christmas fanatic.

Anne Thalmessinger was born in India and came to England when she was ten. She completed a three-year course at art college and then spent 17 happy years as a self-employed studio potter. Later on, she combined working on her own with teaching art in a variety of educational establishments.

Sue Tompkins is now retired after 40 years of paid work encouraging learning in others. She is now finding out how to be a human being in a broader way, which has endless possibilities. She is a keen walker and lives in Grange-over-Sands, Cumbria.

Liz Verlander is a full-time mother and a part-time nurse. She has had a number of pieces published.

Sue Vickerman is a poet and writer with a Christian background. She lives in a Scottish lighthouse and thinks spiritual thoughts whilst looking out of the kitchen window as she washes up.

Christine Vial lives in Enfield, Middlesex, where she teaches literature and creative writing. Her work has been published in a variety of magazines and anthologies and she enjoys reading her work at local poetry groups.

Clare Wallace is 24 and graduated from Bath Spa University with a degree in Cultural Studies and Creative Studies in English. Taking a year out to travel Australia was one of the best years of her life. She secretly wishes she could sing, drive and cook more than cheese on toast.

Tony Walsh is a Manchester-based poet who performs regularly across the UK. He has been published in several magazines and anthologies and his first collection is due to be published by Citizen 32 in 2006.

Tess Ward was a chaplain at the Ark-T Centre in Cowley, Oxford. She is now a chaplain at Nuffield Orthopaedic Hospital in Oxford and is writing a year round book of seasonal prayers celebrating Christian and old Celtic festivals.

Rebecca Warren is 28 years old and lives and works in Solihull. She has had poems published in a number of magazines and anthologies.

Jennifer Waring is 25 and taught ESL in South Korea for two years. She is currently teaching at an elementary school in Seoul and writes children's stories, poetry and non-fiction articles, in between making pretty wall displays.

Jan Waterson has worked in education, health and social care. She is involved with the Small Pilgrim Places Network and in Christian meditation.

Rachel Woodlock is a Muslim feminist from Melbourne, Australia. She has conducted training seminars for young Muslims in Australia and New Zealand for the Islamic Education Trust, co-founded the Cross-Cultural Coffee Group and runs a website on Muslim feminism. She is married and has a daughter.

Bridget Woollard is a photographer who lives in Telford. She circulated 'Seeing differently' in a Christmas letter.

Christine Worsley is an Anglican priest and works as Ministerial and Adult Learning Officer in the Diocese of Ely.

The Iona Community is:

- An ecumenical movement of men and women from different walks of life and different traditions in the Christian church
- Committed to the gospel of Jesus Christ, and to following where that leads, even into the unknown
- Engaged together, and with people of goodwill across the world, in acting, reflecting and praying for justice, peace and the integrity of creation
- Convinced that the inclusive community we seek must be embodied in the community we practise

Together with our staff, we are responsible for:

- Our islands residential centres of Iona Abbey, the MacLeod Centre on Iona, and Camas Adventure Centre on the Ross of Mull

and in Glasgow:

- The administration of the Community
- Our work with young people
- Our publishing house, Wild Goose Publications
- Our association in the revitalising of worship with the Wild Goose Resource Group

The Iona Community was founded in Glasgow in 1938 by George MacLeod, minister, visionary and prophetic witness for peace, in the context of the poverty and despair of the Depression. Its original task of rebuilding the monastic ruins of Iona Abbey became a sign of hopeful rebuilding of community in Scotland and beyond. Today, we are about 250 Members, mostly in Britain, and 1500 Associate Members, with 1400 Friends worldwide. Together and apart, 'we follow the light we have, and pray for more light'.

For information on the Iona Community contact:
The Iona Community, Fourth Floor, Savoy House, 110 Sauchiehall Street,
Glasgow G2 3DH, UK. Phone: 0141 332 6343
e-mail: admin@iona.org.uk; web: www.iona.org.uk

For enquiries about visiting Iona, please contact:
Iona Abbey, Isle of Iona, Argyll PA76 6SN, UK. Phone: 01681 700404
e-mail: ionacomm@iona.org.uk

More resources for Advent & Christmas

Candles & Conifers
Resources for All Saints' and Advent
Ruth Burgess

A collection of seasonal resources – prayers, liturgies, poems, reflections, sermons, meditations, stories and responses – by Iona Community members, associates, friends and others. Covers the weeks from All Saints' Day to Christmas Eve, including saints' days, Remembrance Day, World AIDS Day and Advent. There are liturgies for an outdoor celebration with fireworks, a Christingle service and a longest night service, as well as Advent candle ceremonies and personal prayer practices.

ISBN 978-1-901557-96-1

Hay & Stardust
Resources for Christmas to Candlemas
Ruth Burgess

This companion resource book to *Candles & Conifers* covers the season of Christmastide, including Christmas Eve, Holy Innocents' Day, Winter and New Year, Epiphany, Homelessness Sunday and Candlemas. It also contains eight Christmas plays, including a puppet play.

ISBN 978-1-905010-00-4

Hear My Cry
A daily prayer book for Advent
Ruth Burgess

A daily prayer book for Advent which can also be used as a prayer journal, taking its inspiration from the Advent antiphons – a group of prayers that reflect on the character and activities of God. The format for each day includes a Bible verse, an Advent cry and suggestions for prayer. The pages can be added to and personalised, with line drawings that can be coloured in and space to add your own pictures, reflections and prayers. Instructions for three workshops are also included to enable Advent themes to be explored in a group setting.

ISBN 978-1-901557-95-4

The Jesse Tree

Thom Shuman

We know the familiar stories like Noah and the Ark; we know the famous people, like Mary and David – but what about those people who might only be mentioned once in the Bible (in the lineages in Matthew and Luke)? What about those folks that Jesus might have heard about at bedtime? What about the women, the prophets, the exiles who, while not linked to Jesus genetically, nevertheless passed on their 'spiritual DNA' to him and to us? They are just as much a part of his heritage, his family, his 'tree' as all his relatives by blood and by marriage. They are a part of the tradition and faith we seek to pass onto our children and grandchildren. They are branches on the Jesse tree.

ISBN 978-1-905010-06-6

Cloth for the Cradle

Worship resources & readings for Advent, Christmas and Epiphany

Wild Goose Worship Group

This rediscovery of the stories of Christ's birth through adult eyes contains much to reflect on individually and to use in group and worship situations. The material is drawn from the work of the Wild Goose Resource and Worship Groups whose innovative style of worship is widely admired and imitated.

ISBN 978-1-901557-01-5

Innkeepers and Light Sleepers

Seventeen new songs for Christmas   Songbook/CD

John L Bell

My bonnie boy • He became poor • Christmas is coming • Carol of the Advent • No wind at the window • Justice in the womb • And did it happen • Look up and wonder • God immersed in mystery • Funny kind of night • The pedigree • Ma wee bit dearie • Ho ro ho ro • The aye carol • Simeon's song • Carol of the Epiphany • The refugees

Songbook ISBN 978-0-947988-47-0

CD ISBN 978-1-901557-39-8

Advent Readings from Iona
Brian Woodcock & Jan Sutch Pickard

Celebrate Christmas with reflections and prayers for each day of Advent. This effective antidote to the commercialism of the festive season can be used for individual meditation or group worship. The authors are the former wardens of the Abbey on the Isle of Iona.

ISBN 978-1-901557-33-6

Disturbing Complacency
Lisa Bodenheim

Short, structured readings for each day of Advent, not advocating a 'cosy' view of Christmas but rather urging us to use this season to address some of the most important issues of our time.

ISBN 978-1-905010-37-0

Going Home Another Way
Neil Paynter

Resources for Christmastide to help you hear God's Word through the commercialism of the season, the propaganda of the times; and to glimpse the sacred in the secular.

ISBN 978-1-905010-57-8

Light of the World
Peter Millar & Neil Paynter

Daily readings for Advent from Iona Community members, associates and friends: Peter Millar, John Harvey, Kathy Galloway, Ian M Fraser, David Rhodes, Jan Sutch Pickard and others.

ISBN 978-1-905010-63-9